ICON • THE QUEEN VIC PUB • JONATHAN'S THE RUB • BOADA
É • AMERICAS • SPARROW BAR + COOKSHC
L • PHILIPPE • TINTOS SPANISH RESTAUR
ESON • OPORTO FOOD & WINE BAR • VALEI
VIC & ANTHONY'S STEAKHOUSE • MAX'S WINE DIVE • BENJY'S
OD & WINE BAR • TRULUCK'S • KILLEN'S STEAKHOUSE • UCHI
R, PHOENICIA SPECIALTY FOODS • MONARCH, HOTEL ZAZA •
NDUCA • LIBERTY KITCHEN • GIGI'S ASIAN BISTRO & DUMPLING
ENTINO GELATO • SULLIVAN'S • BISTRO ALEX, HOTEL SORELLA
LERY • BROOKLYN ATHLETIC CLUB • ANVIL BAR & REFUGE •
ABSINTHE • DOUBLE TROUBLE • HUGO'S • BRC • SIMONE ON
NE, ROYAL SONESTA • MASRAFF'S • LINE & LARIAT, HOTEL ICON
• ROOST • GIACOMO'S CIBO E VINO • EL REAL TEX-MEX CAFÉ
REGIS HOTEL • GLASS WALL • FUAD'S • TREVISIO • LE MISTRAL
ALO • DEL FRISCO'S DOUBLE EAGLE STEAKHOUSE • EL MESON
STING ROOM • REEF • MOCKINGBIRD BISTRO WINE BAR • VIC &
OUSE • PLONK! • MARK'S AMERICAN CUISINE • CRÚ FOOD & WINE
RO • QUATTRO, FOUR SEASONS HOTEL • MKT BAR, PHOENICIA
ITALIANO • RISTORANTE CAVOUR, HOTEL GRANDUCA • LIBERTY
• FLUFF BAKE BAR • BACKSTREET CAFÉ • TRENTINO GELATO •
OPPA RISTORANTE ITALIANO • DESSERT GALLERY • BROOKLYN
VEN • RDG • HEARSAY GASTRO LOUNGE • ABSINTHE • DOUBLE
NGOOSE VERSUS COBRA • BLU • TABLEONE, ROYAL SONESTA
JONATHAN'S THE RUB • BOADA CUISINE • ROOST • GIACOMO'S
AR + COOKSHOP • THE REMINGTON, ST. REGIS HOTEL • GLASS
ISH RESTAURANT & WINE BAR • EL GRAN MALO • DEL FRISCO'S
E BAR • VALENTINO, HOTEL DEREK • THE TASTING ROOM • REEF
E • MAX'S WINE DIVE • BENJY'S • DOWN HOUSE • PLONK! • MARK'S
CHI • MONARCH, HOTEL ZAZA • ARTURO'S UPTOWN ITALIANO

HOUSTON
SMALL PLATES
& SIPS

HOUSTON
SMALL PLATES
& SIPS

ERIN M. HICKS

CaptiView™

Houston, Texas

The word "Captiview" and the Captiview logo are trademarks of Captiview, Inc., and are registered in the U.S. Patent and Trademark Office.

U.S. Patent and Trademark Office

ISBN 978-0-9858776-0-6

Text by Erin M. Hicks

Edited by Erin M. Hicks, Taylor Byrne Dodge, Jake Rigdon

Photography by William Jones Miller, Erin M. Hicks

Artwork by William Jones Miller, Jeffrey Linthicum

Production by Erin M. Hicks, William Jones Miller

Based on a design by Erin M. Hicks, William Jones Miller

Printed in China

Published by Captiview, Inc.

Houston, Texas 77007

www.captiview.net

FOR KIT WOHL,
THANKS FOR
BRINGING ME TO
THE PARTY.

SAVORY

SIPS (CONTINUED)

INTRODUCTION

Houston continues to wow the culinary world, rising steadily in the rankings of cities showcasing America's best eats. As exciting as that is, it also creates a bit of a conundrum for gluttonous little piggies like myself, who wake each morning with one burning question on our minds:

"What and where am I going to eat today?!"

With the multitude of fabulous restaurants in town, just deciding where to go can be a daunting task. To make matters worse, once I've chosen a restaurant, there's STILL the commitment to just one menu item, and then the possible 'entree envy' over a companion's selection. As trivial as this seems, thanks to the wave of small plate offerings, I now wake each day with a little less food anxiety.

Small plates may be trending in recent years, but they're hardly a new phenomenon. From French amuse-bouches and Spanish tapas to Greek antipasti, Italian cicchetti and Chinese dim sum, small plates have been around for centuries. I suspect that smaller plates have become so popular in recent years because food lovers want variety. Great for trying out new flavors and exotic ingredients, from local and seasonal to sustainable foods, small plates allow chefs to experiment – and they allow you to create your own tasting menu. In an era when portion sizes seem to be getting bigger and bigger, smaller portions are a refreshing and often healthier choice.

Is healthy indulgence – an oxymoron? I discovered years ago at MAX's Wine Dive, that two of my most favorite things – champagne and french fries – are truly a perfect pairing. The fried, saltiness of the potatoes, cut with Champagne's bright acidity and light bubbles – honestly, there are only a few things that could make me happier. One thing would be if the potatoes were oven-baked instead of deep-fried. Oven-baking takes a little longer, which is often not feasible in a restaurant setting, but certainly is in your own kitchen. With that in mind, I've offered an alternate preparation technique for all of the restaurant dishes in this book that are deep-fried – because that's just how I roll. I'm sure we can agree, that's at least a *healthier* indulgence!

This book was inspired by the chef's tasting/pairing concept, but there's a twist. Instead of the just the traditional food-wine pairing, beer and cocktail pairings are included here, too. And why not? Take the craft beer market, for example. Even if you typically enjoy your beer while gardening or watching the big game, the herbs, spices and fruits in craft beers are a perfect match for some of these unique and simple dishes. It's long been thought, mostly by stuffy sommeliers, that cocktails paired with food are a dining no-no. Where wine coats the palate, cocktails do, in fact, help cleanse the palate and prepare you for the next bite or course. Flavor profiles and varietals are taken into consideration when pairing wine with food. The same holds true with beer and cocktails. It's about linking complementary and contrasting flavors and textures. Do the mixers used in your cocktail pair well with the key ingredients in your dish? Fresh herbs will add brightness and depth to cocktails, and if you were accidentally heavy-handed with the spices in a dish, not to worry – a sweet libation will help temper the heat.

Generally speaking, try to think of cocktails and beer just as you would a great glass of wine – a welcome accompaniment to your dish – not just a way to relax after a long weekend. Thanks to the tips and suggestions of some of Bayou City's world-renowned chefs and wine and spirit professionals, you'll find all that and more in *Houston Small Plates & Sips*.

TINY BUBBLES IN THE WINE
MAKE ME FEEL HAPPY
MAKE ME FEEL FINE

– DON HO

PULLED PORK PANCAKES
TABLEONE, ROYAL SONESTA HOUSTON

PULLED PORK

1 tsp	garlic powder
½ tsp	cumin powder
½ Tbsp	black pepper
¼ tsp	cayenne pepper
1 tsp	onion powder
1¼ tsp	salt
2 to 3 lb	pork loin or a 3 to 4 lb pork shoulder or butt roast (bone-in)

SWEET POTATO PANCAKES

Makes Twelve (3-inch) Pancakes

¾ cup	all-purpose flour
1¾ tsp	baking powder
½ tsp	salt
½ tsp	nutmeg, ground
¾ cup	sweet potato, mashed
1	egg, beaten
¾ cup	milk
2 Tbsp	unsalted butter, melted

BARBECUE SAUCE

1 cup	ketchup
¼ cup	water
2½ Tbsp	apple cider vinegar
2½ Tbsp	brown sugar
1 Tbsp	yellow mustard
½ Tbsp	onion powder
½ Tbsp	garlic powder
¼ tsp	cayenne pepper

fried julienned sweet potatoes, *for garnish*
balsamic glaze, *for garnish*

The ultimate chef's table awaits within The Restaurant at the Royal Sonesta Hotel. Offering commanding views of the action in the kitchen, TableOne guests (up to ten) dine on a menu personally crafted by Chef Peter Laufer, complete with creative wine pairings.

Recipe Notes: Although pork shoulder or butt is most often used for pulled pork, a leaner alternative is pork loin (not tenderloin). A 2- to 3-pound pork loin will yield as much meat as a 3- to 4-pound bone-in pork shoulder or butt roast. If using pork loin, be sure to reserve some of the juice. If the pork seems a bit dry, add some of the juice before you add the barbecue sauce. Chef Laufer believes the barbecue sauce is better if it sits for a day, refrigerated, of course.

YIELD: 6 SERVINGS

For the pulled pork:

Mix all of the spices together. Rub the pork with the spice mixture and refrigerate for at least 1 hour, or overnight.

Preheat the oven to 280°F. Put the pork in a Dutch oven with a lid or wrap the pork in aluminum foil. Place in the oven and cook for 3 to 4 hours (butt or shoulder), or 2½ to 3 hours (loin), or until the internal temperature reaches about 185°F. Remove from the oven and let the pork rest (loosely covered in foil) for at least 10 minutes. Roughly chop, then shred the pork. Pour at least half of sauce on the pork and mix well.

For the sweet potato pancakes:

In a medium bowl, sift together flour, baking powder, salt, and nutmeg. Mix the mashed sweet potatoes, egg, milk and butter in a separate medium bowl. Blend the sweet potato mixture into the flour mixture to form a batter.

Preheat a lightly greased griddle or skillet over medium-high heat. Drop about 2 tablespoons of the batter mixture per pancake and cook until golden brown, about 2 to 3 minutes per side, turning once with a spatula when the surface begins to bubble.

For the barbecue sauce:

Combine all of the ingredients in a saucepan over a low heat. Simmer for 20 minutes, stirring occasionally.

To serve:

Top each pancake with the pulled pork. Garnish with julienned fried sweet potatoes and a drizzle of a balsamic vinegar-maple syrup-reduction (equal parts, cooked low and slow on stovetop).

Wine: A Zinfandel, Malbec or a Texas Syrah
Beer: A pale or amber ale, like Southern Star Bombshell Blonde
Cocktail: Maple Old Fashioned (pg. 134)

VIETNAMESE CRAB SALAD
MASRAFF'S

Masraff's guests are always greeted by at least half of the dynamic father/son team of Tony and Russell Masraff. They make everyone feel like family.

Executive Chef Dominic Juarez continuously seeks out the freshest and unique ingredients from all over the world. A very close relative to the ever popular "Colossal Crab" salad that's been a customer favorite for years, this salad combines two of Chef Juarez's favorite flavors of Houston – Vietnamese and Mexican. This delicious and healthful salad can easily be prepped ahead of time.

Recipe Notes: Don't mix the liquid ingredients with the solid until time of service. Use colossal or jumbo lump crab meat. Romaine hearts should be fresh and crisp. This is also an excellent chopped salad.

YIELD: 6 SERVINGS

For the mango-avocado salsa:

Combine the basil, cilantro and mint in a small bowl. Gently fold in the mango and avocado. Set aside.

For the dressing:

Whisk all of the ingredients together in a small bowl. Pour over the mango-avocado salsa; gently stir to combine.

For the crab-tomato relish:

In a medium bowl, add the tomatoes, crab meat and chives. Drizzle with olive oil and Champagne vinegar. Gently mix to combine. Season with salt, to taste.

To serve:

Spoon some of the mango-avocado salsa into each romaine heart. Top with the crab-tomato relish. Garnish with micro-herbs or parsley leaves.

MANGO-AVOCADO SALSA

1 Tbsp	basil, chopped
1 Tbsp	cilantro, chopped
½ tsp	mint, chopped
1 cup	mango, small dice
1 cup	avocado, small dice

DRESSING

1 Tbsp	white wine vinegar
1 Tbsp	rice wine vinegar
1 tsp	agave nectar
1½ Tbsp	olive oil
¼ tsp	salt
½ tsp	lemon juice

CRAB-TOMATO RELISH

1 cup	cherry tomatoes, thinly sliced
8 oz	colossal or jumbo lump crab meat
1 Tbsp	fresh chives, chopped
2 Tbsp	extra-virgin olive oil
½ Tbsp	Champagne vinegar
to taste	kosher salt
12	hearts of romaine
	micro-herbs or parsley leaves, *for garnish*

Wine: A Riesling from the Alsace region of France
Beer: A raspberry wheat beer, like Abita Purple Haze
Cocktail: 1753 (pg. 124)

HEIRLOOM TOMATO SALAD
LINE & LARIAT, HOTEL ICON

Hotel ICON has had more than a few successful restaurants rotate within its walls, as well as more than a few talented chefs. Line & Lariat is the newest restaurant, and with Executive Chef David Luna at the helm, things are exciting.

This tomato salad is a Mediterranean twist on the southern tomato-cucumber dish, which usually has cucumbers, wedged tomatoes, onion, vinegar and a pinch of sugar. Chef Luna adds feta cheese, toasted pumpkin seeds, basil and mint to the mix; and instead of plain white vinegar, he uses white balsamic vinegar (he's ruined too many dress shirts with splashes of dark balsamic over the years).

Recipe Notes: Chef Luna prefers the creamy texture of Valbreso French feta, which may be found locally at most grocery stores. He says to be sure to choose tomatoes by taste, not by color.

YIELD: 6 SERVINGS

4	large heirloom tomatoes
I pt	grape tomatoes
to taste	salt and pepper
¼ cup	white balsamic vinegar
¼ cup	red onion, julienned
¼ cup	English cucumber, peeled, seeded and diced
I cup	feta cheese, coarsely crumbled
2 Tbsp	pumpkin seeds, toasted
I Tbsp	basil chiffonade
I Tbsp	mint chiffonade
I Tbsp	extra-virgin olive oil

Slice the heirloom tomatoes ¼-inch-thick and halve the grape tomatoes.

Arrange the tomatoes on a platter or individual salad plates.

Season the tomatoes with salt and pepper.

Drizzle the tomatoes with the vinegar.

Scatter the onions, cucumber, feta, pumpkin seeds and herbs over the top.

Drizzle the entire mix with the olive oil and serve immediately.

To toast pumpkin seeds::

Preheat the oven to 375°F and line a baking sheet with parchment paper. Toss clean, dry pumpkin seeds in a bowl with a small amount of olive oil, just enough to coat, and toss with salt. Arrange in a single layer on the parchment paper-lined baking sheet. Bake for 15 to 20 minutes, until golden.

Wine:	A Pinot Grigio
Beer:	A blonde ale or a Texas IPA, like Southern Star Bombshell Blonde or Karbach Hopadillo IPA
Cocktail:	El Gran Exito (pg. 131)

SCOTCH EGG
THE QUEEN VIC PUB

Delicious Indian-British gastropub cuisine, inventive cocktails and a slew of craft beers served in a warm and relaxed atmosphere keep me and a host of Houstonians coming back for more.

Recipe Notes: The Queen Vic's co-owner and Chef Shiva Patel uses her own secret special blend of curry powder, and recommends you use your own favorite curry powder. She prefers to use Pomi tomatoes, which are all-natural, have no added seasonings and may be found at most grocery stores. They are easy to spot in the canned tomato aisle as they come in a box. The Scotch Eggs are deep-fried at The Queen Vic; however, instructions to oven-fry are listed below.

YIELD: 6 SERVINGS

For the Queen's curry:

Add the oil to a saucepot over medium heat and then add the cumin seeds. Sauté until fragrant, about 3 minutes. Add the onions and sauté for 30 to 45 minutes. The onions must cook down and brown, before adding any other ingredients. Add the garlic, ginger, serrano pepper; lower the heat and add the curry powder, stirring to combine. Add the tomatoes and salt and allow to simmer for 30 to 45 minutes. Then add the sugar, cilantro and lemon juice; stir to combine.

For the eggs:

Fill a stockpot with cold water. Add the eggs and bring to a boil. Boil the eggs for 7 minutes, then turn off the heat. Allow to rest for 3 minutes. Peel the eggs under cold water and place in the refrigerator to cool.

For the lamb coating:

In a large bowl, mix the meat thoroughly with the seasonings (serrano through white pepper). Divide the meat into 6 equal portions.

Fill a small bowl with water. Beat the eggs in another small bowl. Add the flour and the Panko to separate, shallow dishes. Dip the boiled eggs into the water, then into the bowl of flour. Carefully and completely cover each egg with the meat mixture. Dip each meat-coated egg into the beaten egg and then cover thoroughly in Panko. Place in the refrigerator for at least 1 hour.

Remove from the refrigerator and preheat the oven to 400˚F. Spray each egg with cooking spray and bake (turning occasionally) until golden brown, 35 to 45 minutes.

To serve:

Cut the eggs in half. Place the egg halves on top of a bed of Queen's curry.

QUEEN'S CURRY

2 Tbsp	olive oil
1 tsp	cumin seeds
5 cups	onion, finely diced
1 Tbsp	garlic, minced
1 Tbsp	ginger, minced
1 Tbsp	serrano pepper, minced
2 Tbsp	curry powder
26 oz	Pomi tomatoes, strained
2½ tsp	salt
¼ tsp	granulated sugar
¼ cup	cilantro, finely diced
2 Tbsp	fresh lemon juice

EGGS

6	eggs

LAMB COATING

1 lb	ground lamb
1 Tbsp	serrano pepper, minced
1 Tbsp	garlic, minced
1 Tbsp	ginger, minced
1 tsp	salt
¼ tsp	coriander powder
¼ tsp	cumin powder
¼ tsp	white pepper
2	eggs, beaten
1 cup	all-purpose flour
2 cups	Panko bread crumbs
	cooking spray or oil, *to oven-fry*

Wine: A Spanish Grenache
Beer: An IPA or an ESB, like Karbach Hopadillo IPA or Fuller ESB
Cocktail: Sachin Tendulkar (pg. 124)

AVOCADO TOMATILLO
JONATHAN'S THE RUB

An epiphanous moment led to the clever naming of Brooklyn-raised Chef Jonathan Levine's restaurant (think Hamlet's "To be or not to be" speech and "rub" as in Texas spice blend). He then spent the next hundred days developing his signature "rub" of about fifteen herbs and spices.

His cooking style is just as clever — simple, familiar ingredients, prepared with a modern twist. This Avocado Tomatillo dish is a perfect example. Avocados are most often served raw and tomatillos — fresh or roasted, are almost always puréed. Flash-sautéed avocado and raw tomatillo slices, mixed with tomatoes, herbs and fresh citrus juices make for a perfect combination of southwestern textures and flavors.

You will also find one of the city's best burgers and lobster rolls at Jonathan's (lobster roll recipe is in my Houston Classic Seafood cookbook).

YIELD: 6 SERVINGS

TOMATILLO SALSA

3	tomatillos
8	cherry tomatoes, quartered
1	yellow bell pepper, julienned
6	basil leaves, julienned
2 Tbsp	parsley, chopped
1	lemon, juiced
1	lime, juiced

AVOCADOS

3	avocados
½ Tbsp	clarified butter
½ Tbsp	extra-virgin olive oil
½ tsp	chipotle powder
	tortilla chips

For the tomatillo salsa:

Remove the husks from the tomatillos and rinse to remove the stickiness. Cut the tomatillos into ¼-inch slices.

In a medium bowl, combine the tomatillos, tomatoes, peppers, basil, parsley, lemon and lime juices.

For the avocados:

Cut the avocados into ½-inch slices.

Heat the butter and olive oil in a sauté pan over medium-high heat. Add the avocado slices and quickly sear. Remove from the heat and sprinkle the avocado slices with chipotle powder.

To serve:

Combine the tomatillo salsa and the avocados. Serve with tortilla chips.

Wine: A New Zealand Sauvignon Blanc
Beer: A light, crisp ale, like Austin (512) Brewing Company (512) Wit
Cocktail: Salt of Life (pg. 132)

CAMARONES HENESY EN HAMACA
BOADA CUISINE

Chef Arturo Boada had a similar dish called Camarones en Hamaca in Cartagena, Colombia at a restaurant owned by David Henesy, who owns many of the best restaurants in Panama City. When Chef Boada returned to Houston, he created this dish, which he calls Camarones Henesy en Hamaca as a tribute to the Panamanian restaurateur.

Recipe Notes: You can buy Goya brand packages of frozen, ripe, already-sliced sweet plantains at most grocery stores — just in case fresh plantains aren't easy to find or ripe enough. For the shrimp, 16/20s, (meaning 16 to 20 shrimp per pound) work well here. Purchasing peeled and deveined shrimp is a real timesaver.

YIELD: 6 SERVINGS

For the plantains:

Thaw the frozen plantains (or if using fresh plantains, peel and slice diagonally into ¾-inch slices). Melt 2 tablespoons of butter in a medium skillet over medium-high heat. Add the plantains, fry until golden on both sides, 2 to 4 minutes. Set aside.

For the shrimp:

In a large skillet, heat the oil over high heat. Add the shrimp and cook for 30 seconds. Add the hearts of palm, capers, tomatoes, garlic, parsley, cilantro, red pepper flakes and sugar and cook for 1 minute, stirring, to combine.

Stir in the chicken broth, soy sauce, ginger juice and wine and cook for an additional minute. Add the remaining butter and stir until incorporated.

To serve:

Place 3 plantain slices on each plate. Top the plantain slices with the shrimp and sauce.

PLANTAINS
18	ripe plantain slices, (about 3 large plantains)
4 Tbsp	unsalted butter, divided

SHRIMP
2 Tbsp	olive oil
18	large shrimp, peeled and deveined
1 cup	hearts of palm, sliced
1⅓ Tbsp	capers
½ cup	tomatoes, diced
1⅓ Tbsp	garlic, chopped
2 Tbsp	parsley, chopped
¼ cup	cilantro leaves
2 tsp	red pepper flakes
¼ tsp	granulated sugar
¼ cup	chicken broth
2 tsp	soy sauce
2 tsp	ginger juice
¼ cup	dry white wine

Wine: A dry Australian Riesling
Beer: An IPA, like Saint Arnold Elissa
Cocktail: Suffering Bastard (pg. 137)

MISO CAULIFLOWER
ROOST

Chef Kevin Naderi's Montrose restaurant popped up nearly overnight and was an instant hit. One of the attractions to Roost is the proficient use of vegetables. This cauliflower recipe has been a favorite of patrons since Roost's doors opened.

Recipe Notes: Chef Naderi flash fries the cauliflower, but I have also included roasting instructions. Bonito flakes are dried sheets of tuna; you can find them at any of the several Asian specialty markets in town.

YIELD: 6 SERVINGS

MISO DRESSING

4 Tbsp	brown/red miso paste
1 cup	mayonnaise
2 tsp	Sriracha Hot Chili Sauce
2 tsp	dark soy sauce
2 Tbsp	clover honey
2 tsp	rice wine vinegar
to taste	salt and pepper

CAULIFLOWER

2	cauliflower heads
	canola oil, *to fry*
	canola or grapeseed oil mister or cooking spray, *to roast*
1 Tbsp	green onions, slivered
2 Tbsp	pine nuts, toasted
handful	bonito flakes, dried

For the miso dressing:

In a large bowl, combine the miso paste, mayonnaise, hot sauce, soy sauce, honey, vinegar, salt and pepper. Whisk until well blended.

For the cauliflower:

Preheat the deep fryer to 375˚F or the oven to 425˚F.

Cut the cauliflower heads into florets.

To fry: When the fryer is to temperature, add the florets and fry until light golden brown and tender, just about 2 minutes. Remove from the fryer and place on a paper towel-lined plate to allow some of the oil to drain.

To roast: Line a sheet pan with aluminum foil. Spray the foil with oil mister or cooking spray. Place florets on the sheet pan and spritz with the oil or cooking spray. Roast for about 20 to 25 minutes, rotating the sheet pan halfway through cooking.

While still hot, add the florets to the dressing. Mix well until the florets are coated. Transfer to a large bowl or platter.

To serve:

Transfer the cauliflower to a large bowl or platter. Top with the green onions and pine nuts and crown with the bonito flakes. Serve immediately.

Wine:	A light-bodied, crisp white, such as an Austrian Grüner Veltliner
Beer:	A Belgian saison, like Brasserie Dupont's Foret
Cocktail:	French 75 with cognac (pg. 133)

GRILLED RADICCHIO
GIACOMO'S CIBO E VINO

Inspired by a visit to northern Italy more than fifteen years ago, this dish was a customer favorite at Lynette Hawkins' old restaurant, La Mora. It was requested by so many of her old customers, it had to be added to the menu at Giacomo's.

This dish hits almost all of the elements of taste. The richness of the creamy mozzarella, the sweetness of the roasted pepper and balsamic vinegar and the saltiness of the prosciutto all contrast beautifully with the bitter radicchio (which is mellowed further by a few minutes on the grill).

Recipe Notes: You can substitute speck for prosciutto to add a rich, smoky flavor, or eliminate the prosciutto altogether for a vegetarian version of this appetizer. Also, make sure the mozzarella is completely encased in the prosciutto so that when it melts, it doesn't spill onto the grill. To separate the radicchio leaves more easily, cut out the stem and scoop out the top core of the head of the radicchio. Then hold it, stem side up, under cold running water, and use the water to help separate the leaves.

YIELD: 6 SERVINGS

12 oz	fresh mozzarella cheese
pinch	salt and pepper
drizzle	extra-virgin olive oil
12	thin prosciutto slices
12	roasted red pepper slices
12	large radicchio leaves
3 cups	wild arugula
drizzle	aged balsamic vinegar

Preheat your grill, grill pan or indoor grill over medium-high heat.

Slice the mozzarella into 1-inch slices. Season the mozzarella with a pinch of salt and pepper. Drizzle with olive oil and wrap in the prosciutto slices.

Slice the peppers into 1- by 2½-inch pieces.

Place a mozzarella bundle on each radicchio leaf, top with a slice of roasted pepper and wrap the leaf around like an envelope.

Grill until hot and the mozzarella is beginning to ooze.

Place on a bed of arugula and drizzle with a little balsamic vinegar.

To roast the bell pepper:

Place 1 large red bell pepper (or 2 small) on a hot grill or under the broiler and cook on all sides until the skin is blistered and charred, about 1 to 2 minutes per side. Place the pepper in a plastic bag or a bowl and cover with plastic wrap. The resulting steam will help separate the skin from the pepper. When the pepper is cool enough to handle, gently scrape the skin off, remove the seeds and membrane, and cut into 12 pieces.

Wine:	An Italian white, rosé or red or a Texas Tuscan-style wine
Beer:	An Italian (or European) pale lager, like Peroni
Cocktail:	Vesper (pg. 125)

CAMPECHANA
EL REAL TEX-MEX CAFÉ

El Real was open for less than a year when it won the 'Best Tex-Mex' award from the Houston Press. That should come as little surprise – it's by the trio of Chef Bryan Caswell, Bill Floyd and Robb Walsh. Chef Caswell was nominated for the James Beard Award for Best Chef Southwest in 2010. He and Floyd co-own the award-winning REEF restaurant and Little Bigs. Walsh was the former restaurant critic for the Houston Press.

Recipe Notes: The El Real kitchen uses 36/40s (meaning 36 to 40 shrimp per pound). Chef Caswell recommends using Texas Shell Shock Shellfish boil, which may be purchased locally at Airline Seafood on Richmond Avenue or online at www.texartfoods.com.

YIELD: 6 SERVINGS

For the cocktail sauce:

Place all of the ingredients for the cocktail sauce (except the cilantro and pico de gallo) in the food processor. Pulse processor until all of the items are incorporated and slightly chunky. Add the cilantro and pico de gallo and stir to combine. Refrigerate until needed.

For the boiled shrimp:

Combine all of the ingredients (except the shrimp) in a large stockpot.

Bring to a boil and then add the shrimp. Cover the pot and turn off the heat. Let the shrimp steep for approximately 5 minutes. Strain, then rinse with cold water. Discard everything but the shrimp.

To serve:

Combine the cocktail sauce and shrimp; mix well. Serve with tostada chips and garnish with avocado slices and lime wedges.

COCKTAIL SAUCE

¼ cup	green olives, chopped
¼ cup	extra-virgin olive oil
⅓ cup	ketchup
½ cup	chile sauce
1 Tbsp	fresh oregano, chopped
1 Tbsp	serrano peppers, chopped
2 Tbsp	fresh lime juice
2½ Tbsp	carrot juice
1 cup	Clamato juice
2 cups	pico de gallo
¼ cup	cilantro, chopped

BOILED SHRIMP

2½	lemons, halved
2½	yellow onions, quartered
1½ Tbsp	kosher salt
1¾ Tbsp	paprika
2½	bay leaves
½ Tbsp	black peppercorns
1 Tbsp	Texas Shell Shock Shellfish Boil (or Creole seasoning)
4 qt	hot water
2½ lb	shrimp, peeled and deveined
	tostada chips
	avocado slices, *for garnish*
	lime wedges, *for garnish*

Wine:	A sweet Texas wine or a Texas High Plains Tempranillo
Beer:	A Mexican lager, like Pacifico
Cocktail:	Skinny Margarita (pg. 131)

BEEF EMPANADAS
AMERICAS

The Cordua family of restaurants has grown exponentially over the last twenty-five years with four different concepts and seven restaurants, which include Americas, Artista, Churrascos and Amazon Grill.

Recipe Notes: La Saltena (frozen empanada dough for baking) may be found locally at Fiesta stores. The empanada filling will be extremely hot, so be patient and allow your empanada to cool before biting into it – your mouth will thank you. The cilantro sauce makes a great dip or salad dressing. I also tested the cilantro sauce recipe substituting Greek yogurt for the mayonnaise – it was quite tasty and the difference in taste negligible.

YIELD: 6 SERVINGS

For the empanadas:

Soak the raisins in the sherry for 1 hour in a bowl. Dice the onion, bell pepper and olives to ¼-inch pieces. Set aside.

Add the olive oil to a large iron skillet and on medium-high heat, sauté the ground beef with bay leaf, cumin, crushed pepper and paprika until it begins to brown. Crumble and render the fat, about 4 to 5 minutes. Add the demi-glace and stir well. Add the oatmeal and cook for a few more minutes, until most of the liquid is absorbed. Add the onion and bell pepper and cook until vegetables are soft. Add olives and raisins and continue for 2 to 3 more minutes. Season to taste with salt and pepper. Spread the mixture evenly onto a baking sheet and allow it to cool in the refrigerator.

Preheat the oven to 375˚F.

Whisk together the egg and water in a small bowl. Scoop about 2 tablespoons of the mixture into the center of each empanada disc. Fold into half-moon shapes and with a wet finger, wipe the edges of the disc. Fold the disc in half carefully. Then, using a fork, seal the empanadas by crimping the edges. Brush the tops of the empanadas with egg wash and sprinkle with a pinch of sugar.

Bake for 25 minutes or until golden brown.

For the cilantro sauce:

Combine all of the ingredients (except mayonnaise) in a small blender or food processor. Purée until completely smooth. Whisk the cilantro purée into the mayonnaise until fully incorporated.

To serve:

Serve the cooled empanadas (halved or whole), with the cilantro sauce.

EMPANADAS

2⅔ Tbsp	California raisins
1½ Tbsp	dry sherry
½ lb	yellow onion
⅓ cup	red bell pepper
2⅔ Tbsp	pimento-stuffed olives
½ Tbsp	olive oil
¾ lb	ground beef
1	bay leaf
¼ tsp	ground cumin
¾ tsp	crushed red pepper
¾ tsp	smoked Spanish paprika
2 Tbsp	beef demi-glace
⅓ cup	oatmeal
to taste	salt and pepper
1	egg
2 Tbsp	water
1	La Saltena Empanada Dough packet (for baking)
1 Tbsp	granulated sugar

CILANTRO SAUCE

1 cup	cilantro leaves
1 Tbsp	jalapeño, chopped
1½ Tbsp	garlic, chopped
2 Tbsp	white vinegar
1 Tbsp	water
½ tsp	salt
1 cup	mayonnaise

Wine: A Malbec
Beer: A Mexican or South American lager, like Cervezas Quilmes from Argentina
Cocktail: Jalapeño Martini (pg. 125)

Sparrow Bar + Cookshop took flight only two short weeks after the quiet closing of t'afia (Chef Monica Pope's restaurant of ten years and in the very same location!).

The restaurant's interior has changed but Chef Pope's mantra remains the same, "Eat where your food lives." Truth be told, farm-to-table in Houston really began with Chef Pope. Simple preparations of local, organic ingredients, picked at the height of ripeness and readiness, is just how she rolls.

Recipe Notes: Use a combination of your favorite garden herbs for this dish. Chef Pope prefers to use local Blue Heron feta, which is super mild, very creamy and not too salty. Blue Heron's products may be purchased locally at most farmer's markets.

1 cup	spiced pecans
⅓ cup	fresh parsley
⅓ cup	fresh tarragon
⅓ cup	fresh rosemary
3	whole wheat phyllo sheets, organic
¼ cup	clarified butter, melted
⅓ cup	feta, crumbled

YIELD: 20 TO 24 PIECES

Finely chop the spiced pecans and herbs.

Place 2 large pieces of plastic wrap on your counter. Place 1 sheet of phyllo on a flat surface.

Brush the top of the phyllo sheet with the melted butter. Scatter with about ⅓ of the pecans and herbs over the buttered sheet, leaving about an inch border.

Brush the top of another layer of phyllo with butter. Place on top of the first layer and again scatter with pecans and herbs. Repeat process for the top layer. Brush the border of the top phyllo sheet with butter once more.

Roll up tightly, lengthwise. Brush the roll with butter, trim any uneven ends and wrap in plastic wrap. Place in the freezer for 3 hours; then cut crosswise into ½-inch slices.

Preheat the oven to 325°F (regular) or 300°F (convection).

Place the slices on a silicone mat or a parchment paper-lined sheet pan. Bake until crispy but light in color, approximately 10 to 12 minutes.

Remove from the oven and sprinkle with the crumbled feta.

Wine:	A Marsanne or a Roussanne
Beer:	A wheat ale, like Karbach Weisse Versa Wheat
Cocktail:	Gin Gin Mule (pg. 128)

PEPPER-CRUSTED GOAT CHEESE
REMINGTON, ST. REGIS HOTEL

Executive Chef John Signorelli's cheese selections shown opposite include his handcrafted, pepper-crusted smoked goat cheese, Point Reyes Toma, caraway cheddar, Cabrales and Teahive - a bergamot oil and black tea-rubbed cheese.

Only rules of an impressive cheese service? Include one cheese from each category: soft, semi-soft, firm or hard, blue and fresh; made from a variety of milk, such as cow, sheep or goat. This creates a pleasant contrast of colors, textures and indulgent flavors.

For cheese service as an appetizer, plan on up to two ounces of each type of cheese per guest. For cheese as a dessert course, you should plan for about an ounce of each cheese per person. Let the cheese come to room temperature (in its wrapper) for at least an hour before serving. However, keep in mind that cheese is easier sliced when cold, so slice it first, re-wrap, and let come it to room temperature.

Serve with quince paste or an apricot compote, chutneys, and dried fruits or fresh fruits such as apple or pear. Warm pistachios, Marcona almonds or nut brittles are also great accompaniments.

YIELD: 1 GOAT CHEESE LOG

3 Tbsp	black peppercorns, cracked/crushed
2 tsp	pink peppercorns, cracked/crushed
to taste	salt
10 oz	chèvre goat cheese log
½ lb	mesquite wood chips
1 Tbsp	lemon-infused extra-virgin olive oil
1½ Tbsp	fresh diced chives, *for garnish* toasted baguettes or artisanal bread

Mix the cracked and crushed peppercorns together, and season with a little salt. Spread the peppercorn mixture on a cutting board. Roll the cheese across the peppercorns, pressing gently to evenly coat.

Put the mesquite wood chips in a foil packet and place in the middle of the outdoor grill or smoker and light on fire. Allow the flames to die down, and the wood chips begin to smolder and smoke.

Place the wire rack with the cheese in the grill or smoker; avoid placing above the heat.

Cover and smoke the cheese for 30 minutes to an hour, depending on desired smokiness.

Remove the cheese, wrap in wax paper, and refrigerate for a day. This will allow the smoky flavor to further penetrate the cheese.

To serve:

Slice the cheese into ¼-inch slices, drizzle with the lemon-infused olive oil and sprinkle the chives over the top. Serve with toasted baguettes or artisanal bread.

Wine:	A southern French Grenache-based red, like a Côtes du Rhône
Beer:	Beer and cheese are best friends – *anything goes!*
Cocktail:	Amaro, (an Italian herbal liqueur) over ice

BLACK TRUFFLE RISOTTO
HUBBELL & HUDSON

Hubbell & Hudson is a foodie's dream: market, bistro, catering service and kitchen. In fact, the only Viking Cooking School in the state is located at Hubbell & Hudson's main location.

Recipe Notes: Chef Austin Simmons uses Swiss Chalet's truffled mushroom paste in this dish (www.swisschalet.com). You may substitute truffle oil for the paste and still achieve a similar taste. He finishes this dish with Hubbell & Hudson's twenty-year aged balsamic vinegar, which is thick and almost syrup-like. You may reduce balsamic vinegar on the stovetop to achieve a similar consistency, but it will not be as rich in flavor.

YIELD: 6 SERVINGS

1½ cups	Arborio rice
4½ Tbsp	shallots, minced
½ Tbsp	garlic, minced
2 Tbsp	extra-virgin olive oil
1 cup	sweet vermouth (sub white wine)
5 cups	chicken stock, low sodium
5 Tbsp	unsalted butter
1¼ cups	Parmesan cheese, grated
2 Tbsp	fresh thyme, minced
2 Tbsp	mushroom truffle paste (sub 2 tsp truffle oil)
to taste	kosher sea salt
to taste	ground white pepper
drizzle	aged balsamic vinegar
	celery leaves, *for garnish*
	shaved Parmesan cheese, *for garnish*

Heat the chicken broth in a medium saucepan over medium-low heat.

Melt half of the butter in a stockpot and add the olive oil. Add the shallots and the garlic; sweat until translucent, about 4 or 5 minutes. Add the rice, and stir continuously for 3 minutes. Deglaze the pan with the vermouth or white wine. Keep stirring, over medium heat, until the wine evaporates.

Add the stock, about ⅓ cup at a time, stirring constantly, until the stock is absorbed from each addition before adding more. Keep adding the stock and stirring until all of it has been absorbed. If the mixture is too thick, add more stock as needed.

Add the remaining butter and the Parmesan, followed by the thyme, and then the truffle paste or oil.

Season to taste with salt and pepper. Drizzle with aged balsamic vinegar.

Garnish with celery leaves and shaved Parmesan. Serve immediately.

Wine: An earthy Syrah-Grenache blend from the Rhone Valley or Paso Robles
Beer: An Imperial stout, like Jester King Black Metal Farmhouse
Cocktail: Harvard (pg. 124)

TOMATO SHRIMP NAPOLEON
GLASS WALL

Famed wine connoisseur André Simon once said, "Food without wine is a corpse; wine without food is a ghost; united and well matched they are as body and soul, living partners."

Food and wine are perfectly united at Glass Wall. Co-owner and grape alchemist Shepard Ross boasts one of the most innovative and value-driven wine lists in town. He believes that a great wine-by-the glass program allows guests to step outside of their comfort zone and try new varietals. He offers fantastic pairing suggestions (by-the-glass) for almost every menu item.

Recipe Notes: Chef Jorge Rodriguez uses Pea Patch beefsteak tomatoes (served at many of the best restaurants in town) and fresh gulf shrimp in this dish. Less ripe tomatoes work best here – especially if you choose to oven-fry them.

YIELD: 6 SERVINGS

For the tomatoes:

Place the tomato slices on a tea towel or paper towels. Whisk the eggs and milk in a medium bowl. Place the flour in a shallow dish. Combine the Panko and parsley in a small mixing bowl; add salt and pepper to taste. Dip each tomato slice in the flour, then in the egg wash to coat, then in the seasoned Panko. Place the Panko-coated tomato slices on a parchment paper-lined baking pan.

To fry: Heat the vegetable oil in a deep fryer or skillet to 350˚F. Add the tomato slices and fry until golden brown, approximately 1 to 2 minutes. Place the fried tomatoes on a rack or paper towel to drain.

To oven-fry: Heat the oven to 425˚F. Place the Panko-coated tomato slices on a rack on a sheet pan. Generously spritz with canola oil or cooking spray. Bake for 10 minutes. Turn the tomatoes over and again spritz with olive oil or cooking spray. Bake for 5 to 10 more minutes.

For the shrimp:

In a medium bowl, combine the shrimp, salt, black pepper, garlic and olive oil. In a sauté pan over medium-high heat, cook the shrimp for 2 to 3 minutes. Remove from the pan and allow to cool. Once cool, dice the shrimp.

For the ravigote:

In a medium bowl, combine the mayonnaise, Worcestershire sauce, Tabasco sauce, buttermilk, capers, garlic powder, onion powder and parsley; mix well.

To serve:

In a medium bowl, combine the diced shrimp and the ravigote; mix well. Place a slice of tomato on a plate, spoon some of the shrimp-ravigote mixture over the tomato, top with another tomato slice. Repeat this process until you have 3 layers. Drizzle with balsamic glaze and garnish with a sprig of rosemary.

TOMATOES

18	beefsteak tomato slices
2	eggs
2 cups	whole milk
1½ cups	unbleached flour
2½ cups	Panko bread crumbs
¼ cup	parsley, chopped
to taste	salt and pepper
	vegetable oil, *to fry*
	cooking spray or oil spritzer, *to oven-fry*

SHRIMP

1½ lb	shrimp, peeled and deveined
1 tsp	salt
1 tsp	black pepper
3	garlic cloves, minced
1 Tbsp	extra-virgin olive oil

RAVIGOTE

1 cup	mayonnaise
1 Tbsp	Worcestershire sauce
½ Tbsp	Tabasco sauce
2 Tbsp	buttermilk
4 Tbsp	capers
1 tsp	garlic powder
1 tsp	onion powder
1 Tbsp	parsley, chopped
drizzle	balsamic glaze
	rosemary sprigs, *for garnish*

Wine:	A dry rosé of Syrah or Monastrell
Beer:	A blonde lager, like Maui Brewing Co. Bikini Blonde Lager
Cocktail:	Gin Blossom (pg. 129)

BLACK FOREST BEEF ROLLS
FUAD'S

Not much has changed at Fuad's since it opened in 1976. Theatrical tableside service ala flambé provides much of the lighting, while piano man Jeff (formerly at River Oaks Grill) croons in the background. Touted as having the largest menu in town (there's no menu!), dining at Fuad's generally begins with Chef Joseph Mashkoori asking what you'd like to eat. He tells you what he has available and then prepares it to exactly to your liking. His hummus, tabouli, lobster bisque and bacon-wrapped, crab-stuffed quail are favorites of many.

Recipe Notes: Thin, rather than thick bacon, works best for this recipe. If you have thick-sliced bacon, not to worry, simply partially cook it in a skillet or in the microwave. For a variation, mix the soy sauce with an equal amount of pineapple juice (or your favorite juice). You can boil the leftover soy sauce mixture, add 1/3 cup of heavy cream, reduce until thickened – then drizzle over the rolls.

YIELD: 18 PIECES

Preheat the oven to 450˚F.

8 oz	beef tenderloin
18	black cherries, pitted
2 oz	cream cheese, cold
1	jalapeño, julienned
9	thin bacon slices
½ cup	soy sauce
18	toothpicks or skewers
drizzle	balsamic vinegar
	fresh jalapeño slices, *for garnish*

Cut the beef into 6 slices. Using a meat mallet, pound out the filet very thinly. Cut the pounded filet into 1- by 2-inch pieces (big enough to wrap around the cherries).

Partially cook your bacon (unless it is really thin) in a skillet or in the microwave (place bacon slices on a plate lined with paper towels, cover and cook for about 1 minute).

Cut the cold cream cheese into pieces small enough to fit inside the cherries.

Stuff each cherry with a piece of cream cheese and a sliver of jalapeño.

Dip each piece of beef into the bowl of soy sauce for a few seconds. Wrap the piece of beef around the cherry and then half a piece of bacon around the beef, securing with a skewer or toothpick.

Place on a sheet pan fitted with a roasting rack and cook for 10 minutes.

Remove the toothpicks from the beef. Drizzle with balsamic vinegar and garnish with sliced jalapeños.

Wine: A Zinfandel from Lodi or Paso Robles
Beer: A Belgian tripel, like Real Ale Devil's Backbone
Cocktail: Where There's Smoke, There's Fire – Sangria (pg. 138)

LEMON CRAB RISOTTO
TREVISIO

Award winning cuisine in a glamorous setting at the Texas Medical Center? You betcha'!

Two mesmerizing sixty-four foot exterior waterfalls, an interior water wall and floor-to-ceiling windows make Trevisio one of the most picturesque restaurants in all of Houston.

Using only the freshest ingredients, native Texan and Executive Chef Jon Buchanan turns out innovative creations as well as classic Italian dishes. He's a three-time award winner at the annual International Risotto Festival – not bad for a former Air Force fly boy – and this is the recipe that earned him top honors!

Recipe Notes: Don't use a metal spoon to stir the risotto as it will break the rice grains. For a variation, top the dish with grilled shrimp.

YIELD: 6 SERVINGS

For the risotto:

Add the olive oil to a stainless steel pot over medium heat. Sauté the shallots and garlic until slightly translucent, about 3 to 5 minutes. Add the rice and continue to sauté over medium heat until the rice develops a nutty aroma, about 3 to 5 minutes. Deglaze the pan with white wine. Stir until the wine is almost absorbed and then add ½ cup of the hot stock while constantly stirring. When the stock is almost absorbed, add another ½ cup of stock. Continue stirring and repeat this process until all the stock has been added and absorbed. Stir in the heavy cream and the cheese. Add the lemon juice and zest. Season with salt and pepper.

For the lemon butter-crab sauce:

In a stainless steel saucepot, sauté the shallots and garlic in olive oil until slightly soft. Add the white wine, peppercorns, bay leaves and reduce by half. Next, add the heavy cream and reduce by half. Once reduced, remove from the heat and whisk in the butter a few pieces at a time until all of the butter has been incorporated. Add the lemon juice and season with salt and pepper. Strain the sauce to remove the solids and return to a clean saucepot. Add the crab meat and slowly reheat the crab in the sauce over low heat.

To serve:

Top each serving of risotto with the lemon butter-crab sauce. Garnish with chopped chives.

RISOTTO

¼ cup	extra-virgin olive oil
¼ cup	shallots, chopped
1 Tbsp	garlic, chopped
1½ cups	Arborio rice
2 cups	white wine
6 cups	chicken stock, hot
½ cup	heavy cream
½ cup	Grana Padano cheese, grated
2	lemons, juiced
1	lemon, zest of
to taste	salt and pepper

LEMON BUTTER-CRAB SAUCE

1	shallot, chopped
1	garlic clove, chopped
1 tsp	extra-virgin olive oil
½ cup	white wine
1 tsp	black peppercorns
2	bay leaves
½ cup	heavy cream
¾ cup	unsalted butter, small dice
1	lemon, juiced
to taste	salt and pepper
1 lb	jumbo lump crab meat
	chopped chives, *for garnish*

Wine:	A clean, (no oak) Italian white from Friuli or Campania
Beer:	A German wheat beer, like Paulaner Hefe-Weizen
Cocktail:	Gin Gin Mule (pg. 128)

WILD MUSHROOM CRISPS
LE MISTRAL

It's not surprising that Le Mistral co-owner and Chef David Denis is certified as a Master-Level Chef by the Culinary Institute of America — he and his brother, Sylvain (co-owner and sommelier) come from two generations of chefs and restaurateurs.

Recipe Notes: Chef Denis uses a combination of yellow feet, porcini and black trumpet mushrooms in this dish, but you may use any type you like. Your mushrooms will have a better flavor if they are golden and crispy. Don't build the dish too early before serving, or it will become soggy. For a rich and decadent variation, use the same technique but add another layer with duck confit.

YIELD: 12 CRISPS

For the mushroom sauté:

Clean the mushrooms with a damp towel – do not wash your mushrooms under water. Peel and separate the black trumpet mushrooms by hand, slice the porcini ¾-inch thick, and leave the yellow feet whole.

Heat the butter and oil in a medium-sized sauté pan over medium-high heat. Add the mushrooms and season with salt and pepper. Sauté until golden brown, and then add the shallots, garlic and fresh thyme.

For the sauce:

Heat a small pot over medium heat. Add 1 tablespoon of the butter, the shallots and the sage and cook until light brown in color. Deglaze with the port wine, increasing the heat to medium-high and cook until the liquid is reduced by half. Add the veal stock and cook until the liquid is again reduced by half. Pass through a sieve. Place the liquid back into the saucepan. Incorporate the remaining butter into the liquid. Add salt and pepper to taste.

For the phyllo crisps:

Preheat the oven to 375°F. Using kitchen scissors or a knife, cut your phyllo sheets into 3-inch squares. Incorporate the egg yolk into the melted butter. Lay out a silicone mat on a sheet pan. Brush the butter-egg-yolk-mixture on top of this layer and place another layer of phyllo on that. Repeat this process until you have 6 layers of phyllo. Bake until they are a light golden color, approximately 2 to 4 minutes.

To serve:

Separate some of the phyllo layers so that you get 2 to 3 layers from each square. The layers should be crispy, so rebake for a minute or so, if necessary. Top a layer with about a tablespoon of the mushroom sauté. Add another phyllo layer and repeat this process until you have 3 layers. Drizzle the sauce on top and enjoy.

MUSHROOM SAUTÉ

2 lb	mushrooms
1 Tbsp	unsalted butter
1 Tbsp	extra-virgin olive oil
to taste	sea salt and pepper
2 Tbsp	shallots, finely diced
1 tsp	garlic, thinly sliced
1 Tbsp	fresh thyme, chopped

SAUCE

2 Tbsp	unsalted butter, divided
2	shallots, sliced
1	sage sprig
1 cup	port wine
2 cups	veal stock
to taste	salt and pepper

PHYLLO CRISPS

6	phyllo sheets
2 Tbsp	clarified butter, melted
1	egg yolk, beaten

Wine: A Pouilly-Fumé or a white Bordeaux; Côtes du Rhône
Beer: An oak-aged pale ale, like Buffalo Bayou Whiskey Barrel Aged 1836
Cocktail: Purple Mule (pg. 138)

LAMB MEATBALLS
PHILIPPE RESTAURANT + LOUNGE

Executive Chef and owner Philippe Schmit now has a new title to his name: Maîtres Cuisiniers de France. Philippe was one of only ten French chefs in the United States to garner the prestigious honor in 2012, and the only chef in Texas.

And the accolades don't stop there – Food & Wine magazine named beverage director Vanessa Treviño Boyd one of the Top Sommeliers of 2012 and the French restaurant was Houston's only representative on Wine Enthusiast's 100 Best Wine Restaurant list.

This dish was inspired by two former French colonies, Morocco and Tunisia. Often used in North African cooking, harissa is a hot chili sauce made from a combination of piri piri, serrano and other chili peppers, as well as garlic and spices. If, after preparing this dish, you realize harissa is a new favorite of yours, be sure to check out the harissa olive oil at Olive and Vine.

Recipe Notes: Make sure to use a powerful blender for the harissa sauce. Otherwise, you'll have to strain the sauce to eliminate the red pepper skins. The meatballs will shrink slightly after cooking. You can substitute sausage-pork mix for the lamb and tomato sauce for the harissa. Remember that lamb and mint are a classic combination – serve with store-bought mint chutney, if desired.

YIELD: 30 MEATBALLS

For the harissa ketchup:

Add the olive oil to a saucepot over medium-low heat and sweat the peppers and garlic cloves for about 10 minutes. Add the cumin, coriander, harissa paste, tomato paste, tomatoes, jalapeño and stir to combine. Let simmer for 5 minutes; season with salt and pepper, to taste. Purée the mixture in a blender; then add the extra-virgin olive oil to make the harissa sauce. Combine the sauce and the ketchup and mix well.

For the meatballs:

Preheat the oven to 400°F.

Combine all of the ingredients in a bowl and mix well with your hands. Form into small meatballs, approximately ¾-inch diameter. Place the meatballs on a half sheet pan and bake for 15 minutes. Let cool for a few minutes, then skewer and coat the meatballs with the harissa ketchup.

To serve:

Serve with mint chutney, if desired.

HARISSA KETCHUP

½ Tbsp	olive oil
1 cup	red bell pepper, diced
1½	garlic cloves, minced
⅛ tsp	ground cumin
⅛ tsp	ground coriander
2 Tbsp	harissa paste
½ Tbsp	tomato paste
½ cup	fresh tomatoes, diced
½	jalapeño, chopped
to taste	salt and pepper
1 Tbsp	extra-virgin olive oil
1 cup	ketchup

MEATBALLS

1¼ lb	ground lamb
¼ cup	roasted red bell pepper, finely diced
¼ cup	red onion, finely diced
1½	roasted garlic cloves, puréed
¾ tsp	Cajun seasoning
¾ tsp	dried oregano
1½ Tbsp	harissa paste
¼ tsp	ground cumin
to taste	salt and pepper
2 tsp	fresh mint, chopped
2 tsp	fresh parsley, chopped
30	skewers

Wine: A rustic Rhone
Beer: A dark ale, like Real Ale Brewhouse Brown Ale
Cocktail: French Cowboy (pg. 135)

STUFFED PIQUILLO PEPPERS
TINTOS SPANISH RESTAURANT & WINE BAR

Introduced by Spaniards' new world travels to the Caribbean Islands, piquillo peppers are grown mainly in northern Spain. The Spanish word for "little beak", piquillos have a unique, spicy-sweet flavor and are perfect for tapas. They can be stuffed with almost anything, including ground or shredded beef or chicken, shrimp, seafood, and/or any soft cheese – just drizzle with some olive oil and a little salt and pepper. They are also very nutritious – loaded with Vitamins C, A, E and B.

Recipe Notes: You can find piquillo peppers canned or jarred at most grocery stores, including Spec's, Fiesta and HEB's Central Market. Handle the piquillos carefully so they don't break. Also, be sure to drain and pat dry before stuffing.

YIELD: 12 PIECES

12	piquillo peppers
2 cups	fresh spinach
1 tsp	olive oil
8 oz	goat cheese, room temperature
2 Tbsp	parsley, chopped
¼ cup	shallots, minced
1 Tbsp	pine nuts, toasted
drizzle	extra-virgin olive oil
	balsamic glaze, *for garnish*
	chopped fresh parsley, *for garnish*

Remove the peppers from the can or jar and pat dry.

Chop the spinach. Heat a little olive oil in a small skillet over medium-high heat. Add the spinach and cook, just until wilted. Drain any water from spinach.

In a medium-sized bowl, combine the cheese, parsley, shallots, pine nuts and spinach, making sure all of the ingredients are evenly distributed.

Carefully fill each pepper with about a tablespoon of the cheese mixture. It's easiest to fill the peppers with a piping bag or a makeshift plastic piping bag (place the softened cheese in a plastic bag, remove air, seal and cut a bottom corner off the bag).

To serve:

You may serve these cold or heat them in a 350°F oven for 3 to 5 minutes, just until the cheese is soft and melting. Drizzle with your favorite virgin olive oil and balsamic glaze. Garnish with chopped parsley.

To toast pine nuts:

Preheat the oven to 375°F. Spread the pine nuts on a baking sheet. Place in the oven, stirring occasionally, until golden-brown, about 5 to 10 minutes.

Wine:	A fruity and floral white, like a Spanish Albarino
Beer:	A pilsner lager, like Estrella Damm Inedit
Cocktail:	Purple Mule (pg. 138)

DIABLOS A CABALLOS
EL GRAN MALO

El Gran Malo, which means "the big bad" in Spanish, is everything but bad.

Chef Greg Lowry's gastrocantina-inspired bites pair perfectly with their creative cocktails, made from over fifty house-crafted seasonal and unique tequila infusions, such as roasted Texas pecan with sea salt and cayenne pepper, strawberry-cucumber and vanilla habanero.

Bacon-wrapped, but stuffed with the gourmand combination of gorgonzola and goat cheese, it's rumored that Houston Chowhounds founder Jenny Wang likes to top Malo's torta burger with these jalapeños!

YIELD: 18 STUFFED JALAPEÑOS

For the melon gastrique:

In a medium saucepan over high heat, add all of the ingredients. Cover and bring to a boil. Reduce heat to medium-high and continue to cook covered, stirring occasionally for about 20 minutes, until the mixture is reduced by half and is a syrup-like consistency. Purée the mixture using an immersion blender or a blender.

For the jalapeños:

Preheat oven to 425°F.

Slice the jalapeños in half lengthwise. Using a spoon, gently scrape out the seeds and membranes. In a small bowl, combine the goat cheese and the Gorgonzola. Fill the jalapeños with the cheese mixture, using a spoon or a piping bag. You can use a zippered plastic bag as a makeshift piping bag (place the softened cheese in a plastic bag, remove air, seal and cut a bottom corner off the bag). Cut the bacon strips in half. Wrap a piece of bacon around each jalapeño, and secure with a toothpick. Place the wrapped jalapeños on a baking sheet. Bake for 20 to 25 minutes, or until the bacon is done. If the bacon does not look done enough, you may finish under the broiler for a few minutes.

To serve:

Place the jalapeños on a platter or individual plates. Drizzle with the melon gastrique and garnish with Cotija cheese.

MELON GASTRIQUE

½	fresh jalapeño, julienned
¾ cup	cantaloupe, diced
2 Tbsp	Champagne vinegar
2 Tbsp	white onion, chopped
2 Tbsp	granulated sugar
¾ cup	apple, peeled and diced
1 tsp	paprika
pinch	salt and black pepper

JALAPEÑOS

9	fresh jalapeños
6 oz	goat cheese, softened
6 oz	Gorgonzola cheese, softened
9	bacon strips
18	toothpicks
¼ cup	crumbled Cotija cheese, *for garnish*

Wine: A Viognier or a Texas Gewürztraminer
Beer: A blonde ale, like Real Ale Firemans #4
Cocktail: Strawberry Cucumber Margarita (pg. 130)

GRILLED PARMESAN OYSTERS
DEL FRISCO'S DOUBLE EAGLE STEAKHOUSE

With so many garlic-flavored dishes on the menu, the grilled Parmesan oysters fit right in at Del Frisco's Double Eagle Steakhouse – and they help pay tribute to its Cajun roots.

Recipe Notes: For starters, look for the freshest, plumpest oysters. When preparing the mixture, don't let it sit too long, and try to bake the oysters immediately to avoid letting the mixture thicken. Use rock salt to help stabilize the oysters on the baking sheet and also for serving, if necessary. For a variation of this simple dish, try adding some sautéed spinach into the butter mixture.

YIELD: 6 SERVINGS

GARLIC BUTTER SAUCE

¼ lb	unsalted butter
1 Tbsp	fresh garlic, minced
½ oz	Tabasco sauce
¼ tsp	black pepper
¾ tsp	Worcestershire sauce
½ Tbsp	fresh lemon juice

OYSTERS

24	oysters, shucked on half shell
½ cup	Parmesan cheese, grated
	lemon wedges, *for garnish*
	Tabasco sauce, *for garnish*

For the garlic butter sauce:

Melt the butter in a saucepan over low heat and add the garlic, Tabasco sauce, black pepper, Worcestershire sauce and lemon juice. Remove from the heat.

For the oysters:

Preheat the oven to broil, and set the rack about 6 to 8 inches from the broiler.

Place the oysters on a baking sheet making sure that they are level (rock salt is useful to help stabilize the oysters).

Add a teaspoon of the garlic butter sauce to each oyster, and top with a teaspoon of grated Parmesan.

Broil in the oven until a light golden brown color is achieved, about 10 minutes.

To serve:

Arrange the oysters on a platter. Garnish with lemon wedges and additional Tabasco sauce, if desired.

Wine:	A California Chardonnay or a dry Champagne
Beer:	A stout, like Southern Star Buried Hatchet
Cocktail:	French 75 (pg. 133)

TORTILLA ESPAÑOLA
EL MESON

Chef Peter Garcia says there are five things that a Spanish man must know how to do well: play soccer and guitar, paint, kiss and make a proper Spanish Tortilla (omelette). His father was famous for his Tortilla Española, both in Manhattan and also in Cuba, where he never appeared at a party or picnic without a tortilla. It was a very Spaniard thing to do in Cuba and sort of became his "calling card."

Peter learned how to make a proper Spanish Tortilla in the kitchen of his father's Manhattan restaurant. I received my proper tortilla lesson in the very hot kitchen at El Meson, which, after a long night of drinking mezcal, was an experience I will never forget.

Recipe Notes: The traditional way to prepare the tortilla is with fried potatoes, however, I've also included instructions on how to oven-fry the potatoes. Add your favorite fresh herbs to the tortilla, if you like.

YIELD: 6 SERVINGS

For the potatoes:

To fry: Heat the oil over medium-high heat in a large skillet. Add the potatoes and fry in the oil, turning the heat down just enough so that the oil still bubbles around the edge. You want to brown the potatoes on the outside then again reduce the heat so the potatoes will cook all the way through. Remove from the heat. Transfer to a large mixing bowl and cool in the refrigerator

To oven-fry: Preheat the oven to 425°F. Line a sheet pan with parchment paper. Put the potatoes in a medium-sized bowl and drizzle with olive oil. Toss to coat well. Place the potatoes on the sheet pan and bake for about 25 to 30 minutes, or until golden brown, rotating the sheet pan after about 10 minutes. Then flip the potatoes.

For the onions:

Cut the onions into a rough ½-inch dice. Heat the olive oil in a skillet over medium-high heat. Add the onions and reduce the heat to medium-low. Sweat the onions for 15 to 20 minutes until very light golden brown. Remove from the heat and add the black pepper. Add fresh herbs now, if desired. Remove from the heat and add to the potatoes. Refrigerate until cool.

Add the whisked eggs to the cooled potatoes and onions. Add the sea salt and garlic; fold over with a spoonula to make sure everything is coated with the eggs .

Heat the olive oil in a deep 8-inch non-stick skillet over medium-high heat, making sure the sides of the skillet are also coated with oil. Lower the heat to medium and add the egg mixture. Using a spatula, evenly spread out the ingredients. Cook for 10 minutes, jiggling the skillet every so often to help prevent sticking. Placing a plate or platter over the skillet, invert the skillet to release the tortilla, then slide back into the skillet to cook the bottom. Press down on the top of the tortilla to deflate a bit and cook for an additional 10 minutes.

To serve:

Let the tortilla sit for 15 to 20 minutes, as it needs time to rest. Cut into wedges and serve at room temperature. Garnish with Spanish olives, if desired.

Wine:	A medium-bodied red with light tannins, like a Rioja Crianza
Beer:	A dry, crisp lager, like Carta Blanca
Cocktail:	Que Me Quentas (pg. 131)

POTATOES

2	large russet potatoes
¼ cup	extra-virgin olive oil, *to fry*
drizzle	extra-virgin olive oil, *to oven-fry*

ONIONS

2	medium onions
2 Tbsp	extra-virgin olive oil
½ tsp	pepper
5	eggs, whisked
½ tsp	coarse sea salt
1	garlic clove, minced
1 Tbsp	extra-virgin olive oil
	Spanish olives, *for garnish*

STUFFED DATES
ALTO PIZZERIA

Chef Robert Del Grande is known for his diversified offerings with menu items stemming from French and Spanish backgrounds. These stuffed Medjool dates are another example of his eclectic culinary taste.

Recipe Notes: Speck comes pre-packaged and sliced and is sold in most grocery stores behind the deli counter. You may substitute prosciutto, pancetta or even bacon for the speck.

YIELD: 24 DATES

For the dates:

Split each date lengthwise and remove the stone. Stuff an almond into each date-half. Cut the speck slices lengthwise, into 1- by 2½-inch pieces. Wrap each stuffed-date-half with a piece of speck, securing with a pick or toothpick.

For the gastrique:

Mix the sugar and the vinegar in a saucepan and simmer over medium heat until the mixture is reduced by half (this will take at least 10 minutes). Add the crushed peppercorns and adjust to low heat for 2 minutes, allowing mixture to continue to simmer. Remove from the heat and let cool to room temperature.

To serve:

Heat the oven to 400°F.

Place the dates on a greased baking sheet, with the cut ends facing up, and bake for 3 to 4 minutes. Remove the dates from the oven and arrange on a serving plate. Drizzle the gastrique over the dates using a large spoon. Sprinkle the Gorgonzola over and around the dates. Garnish with parsley leaves.

DATES
12	Medjool dates
24	smoked almonds
12	speck slices (2 oz)

GASTRIQUE
½ cup	granulated sugar
½ cup	Champagne vinegar
1 Tbsp	pink peppercorns, crushed
½ cup	Gorgonzola cheese, crumbled
24	picks or toothpicks parsley leaves, *for garnish*

Wine: A Roussanne or a white northern Rhône; an aged Rioja

Beer: An amber or Belgian strong ale, like Saint Arnold Amber or Unibroue Terrible

Cocktail: Maple Old Fashioned (pg. 134)

SPINACH ARTICHOKE CROSTINI
OPORTO FOOD & WINE BAR

Oporto Food & Wine Bar's selection of Euro-Mediterranean inspired tapas and wine list (over fifty wines by-the-glass) is said to be like going to Europe without a passport.

Recipe Notes: Spinach and artichoke dips make for easy assembly when entertaining. This recipe was tested using both fresh and also high quality frozen spinach – the difference in taste was negligible. The mix can be used for other preparations like stuffed portobellos or simply as a dip, but it's slightly more elegant served as crostini. If you're not a garlic lover, you might want to use a little less than what's called for here.

YIELD: 18 CROSTINI

Preheat oven to 350˚F.

Drain and rinse the artichokes. Allow to drain on a paper towel or squeeze them dry.

Bring a large pot of water to a boil over high heat. Put ice cubes and water in a large bowl. Boil the spinach for 30 seconds to 1 minute. Drain the spinach and plunge into the ice water. Leave in the ice bath for a few minutes to stop the cooking process. Squeeze the spinach dry.

Rough chop the artichokes and spinach; set aside.

In a medium bowl, combine the onion, garlic, salt, pepper, sour cream, mayonnaise and ⅓ cup of the Parmesan; mix well. Add the spinach and artichokes last; stir gently to combine.

Bias-cut the baguette into ¼-inch slices. Place the baguette slices on a sheet pan. Toast for 3 to 4 minutes and remove from oven.

Mound the spinach and artichoke mixture on top of each crostini. Sprinkle with the remaining Parmesan cheese.

Bake for 5 to 7 minutes, or until the Parmesan crisps. Garnish with a strip of roasted red bell pepper, if desired.

¾ cup	artichokes, canned
4½ cups	fresh spinach (10 oz)
¼ cup	red onion, diced
2½ tsp	garlic, minced
⅓ tsp	salt
⅓ tsp	black pepper
⅓ cup	sour cream
¼ cup	Hellmann's mayonnaise
½ cup	Parmesan cheese, grated, divided
1	fresh baguette
	roasted red bell pepper strips, *for garnish*

Wine: An Albarino; or a Spanish Tempranillo
Beer: A wheat beer, like Buffalo Bayou Hibiscus Wit
Cocktail: Argentini (pg. 125)

PORTOBELLO MUSHROOM
VALENTINO, HOTEL DEREK

Valentino is always evolving. Since their start in 1972 in Santa Monica, each chef-led kitchen has had a different take on ingredients and flavors. The menus change over time as palates change, but always maintain a fresh attitude and Italian roots.

Chef Cunninghame West started cooking mushrooms similar to this almost fifteen years ago, in San Francisco. Also great on a sandwich, this dish has evolved through the years.

Recipe Notes: When picking out mushrooms, always look for ones that are firm and thick. They'll take more time to cook through, but only because they have more meat to them. Cover the dish while baking to eliminate any texture change — it will steam and be soft throughout. If you don't love the bite of fresh garlic, be sure to add a little less than what's called for.

PAPRIKA-BASIL AIOLI

1 cup	mayonnaise
15	large basil leaves, chiffonade
5	garlic cloves, chopped
1 Tbsp	Parmesan cheese, grated
½ Tbsp	pine nuts
1 Tbsp	paprika
to taste	salt and pepper

MUSHROOMS

6	large portobello mushrooms
2 Tbsp	balsamic vinegar
2 Tbsp	extra-virgin olive oil
to taste	salt and pepper
2	large rosemary sprigs

YIELD: 6 SERVINGS

For the paprika-basil aioli:

Blend the mayonnaise with the basil, garlic, Parmesan, pine nuts in a food processor or blender, adding the paprika a little at a time until the desired color and flavor is reached. Season with salt and pepper, to taste.

For the mushrooms:

Preheat the oven to 325˚F.

Remove the stems from the mushrooms. Place the mushrooms on a baking pan, splash them with balsamic vinegar and olive oil (Chef West likes to lightly fill the stem space with olive oil); add salt and pepper, to taste. Place the rosemary sprigs over the top and add some water to cover the bottom of the pan.

Bake until cooked through, 7 to 10 minutes. Be careful to not overcook, as the mushrooms will shrink and may get chewy.

To serve:

Slice the mushrooms in half, arrange on a plate and serve with the paprika-basil aioli.

Wine:	An earthy Pinot Noir
Beer:	A Belgian strong ale, such Chimay Grand Réserve
Cocktail:	French 75 with cognac (pg. 133)

BRIE MOSTARDA
THE TASTING ROOM

The Tasting Room's menu emphasizes shareable plates in a comfortable and communal atmosphere, paired with superb wines from around the world. They have live music several nights a week, multiple locations around town — and all sell retail wine to-go!

Mostarda is an Italian chutney-like condiment made with varied types and combinations of dried fruits and mustard seeds that dates back to the 1600s. The best known variation of mostarda comes from Italy's Cremona (mostarda di Cremona), which is also produced commercially. Other uses for mostarda include serving with pâté, sausages, grilled and roasted meats, pasta and even seafood.

Recipe Notes: Use your favorite combination of dried fruits (and even a little fresh fruit). If you cannot find Baby Belletoile, be sure to use good quality brie.

YIELD: 6 SERVINGS

For the mostarda:

Combine all of the ingredients in non-reactive pan over medium-high heat. Cover the pan and bring to a boil. Reduce to a simmer and cook until all of the liquid is absorbed, about 10 to 15 minutes. Remove the pan from the heat and cool.

To serve:

Preheat oven to 350˚F.

Put the cheese and the mostarda in an oven-proof container and place in the oven. Bake until the brie is melted and bubbling, about 10 minutes. Serve with sliced baguette or crackers.

MOSTARDA

½ cup	dried cherries
¼ cup	dried figs, chopped
¼ cup	dried apricots, chopped
¼ cup	dried cranberries, chopped
2 Tbsp	honey
1 Tbsp	shallot, chopped
1 cup	white wine
1 Tbsp	Champagne vinegar
1 Tbsp	light mustard seeds
16 oz	Baby Belletoile Brie
	sliced baguette or crackers

Wine: A Viognier; a Pinot Noir or a brut Champagne
Beer: A Belgian Trappist, like Chimay Première (Red)
Cocktail: B_2 (pg. 139)

Chef Bryan Caswell personally served my first shrimp shooter, which he gleefully topped off with a shot of Dripping Springs vodka – very Bloody Mary-esque. Be sure to use at least two-ounce shot glasses if you want to serve with added vodka.

Recipe Notes: For the shrimp, boil peeled and deveined 16/20s in your favorite boiling spice or pick up a bag of Texas Shell Shock Boiling Spice locally at Airline Seafood on Richmond Avenue or order online at www.texartfoods.com.

CONSOMMÉ

6 oz	horseradish root
1⅛ cups	white vinegar
¾ cup	ketchup
½ tsp	Worcestershire sauce
1½ tsp	salt
½ tsp	granulated sugar
1½ tsp	Tabasco sauce
1⅓ cups	water
3 Tbsp	fresh lemon juice
1	cucumber, brunoise
1	avocado, brunoise
18	shot glasses
18	shrimp, boiled, peeled and deveined
	micro-herbs, *for garnish*

YIELD: 6 SERVINGS

For the consommé:

Peel and grate the horseradish. Soak the horseradish in a bowl of vinegar for 1 hour.

Add the horseradish/vinegar mixture and the remaining ingredients to a blender and pulse until well combined. Pour into a cheesecloth-lined sieve and refrigerate overnight. Discard everything but the remaining liquid. Refrigerate until ready to use.

To serve:

Pour about 2 tablespoons of consommé into each shot glass. Add a teaspoon each of the cucumber and avocado brunoise. Top each shot glass with a boiled shrimp Garnish with micro-herbs, if desired. Keep chilled until ready to serve.

To brunoise the cucumber and avocado:

First peel and de-seed both the cucumber and avocado. Cut into long thin strips, like matchsticks (also known as julienne), then turn a quarter and dice again.

Wine:	A Texas Viognier
Beer:	A Mexican lager, like Pacifico
Cocktail:	Top the Shrimp Shooters with Dripping Springs vodka

BRAISED SHORT RIB
MOCKINGBIRD BISTRO WINE BAR

Named for the state bird of Texas, Mockingbird Bistro Wine Bar is one of the city's most acclaimed eateries, known for its American and French bistro fare – all made with a Texas twist. Executive Chef and owner John Sheely encourages creativity in the kitchen and updates the menu seasonally. Diners love sitting on the red velvet stools along the marble-topped bar to enjoy the bar bites, wine and cocktail selections, which are some of the best in town.

Recipe Note: Chef Sheely noted that these rich, tender short ribs can be made a day ahead; just reheat with the jus.

YIELD: 6 SERVINGS

For the short ribs:

Preheat the oven to 325˚F.

Heat the olive oil in a heavy, large ovenproof pot over medium-high heat. Sprinkle the ribs with kosher salt and pepper. Working in batches, add the ribs to the pot and brown well, turning often, about 8 minutes per batch. Remove the seared ribs from the pot; set aside.

Pour off all but 2 tablespoons of the drippings from the pot. Add the chopped onion, carrot and celery and cook over medium-low heat until the vegetables are soft, stirring frequently, about 10 minutes. Add the garlic and herbes de Provence; stir for 1 minute. Add the wine and 2 cups of the broth; bring to a boil over high heat, scraping up any browned bits. Add the tomato paste and bay leaf. Return the ribs and any accumulated juices to the pot. If needed, add the remaining broth and/or water to the pot to barely cover the ribs. Bring to a boil. Add the zest. Cover the pot tightly and transfer to the oven.

Bake until the ribs are very tender, stirring occasionally, about 2½ hours.

For the polenta:

Bring the chicken stock to a boil in a large saucepan. Reduce the heat to medium-low; slowly whisk in the cornmeal. Cook, stirring often, until the cornmeal is very soft, thick and creamy, about 20 minutes. Remove from the heat. Add the Parmesan and the butter, and stir until melted. Season with salt and pepper, to taste.

To serve:

Spoon some polenta into a bowl. Top with a short rib and some jus.

SHORT RIBS

2 Tbsp	olive oil
6 lb	meaty beef short ribs
to taste	salt and pepper
1	large onion, finely chopped
1	medium carrot, finely chopped
1	celery stalk, finely chopped
12	garlic cloves, peeled
1 Tbsp	dried herbes de Provence
2 cups	Zinfandel (red)
2½ cups	veal stock or beef broth
3½ Tbsp	tomato paste
1	bay leaf
1	orange, zested
1	lemon, zested

POLENTA

4½ cups	chicken stock (low sodium)
1½ cups	yellow cornmeal
½ cup	Parmesan Reggiano cheese, grated
1½ Tbsp	unsalted butter
to taste	salt and pepper

Wine: A California Cabernet Sauvignon
Beer An American IPA, like Rahr & Sons Stormcloud IPA
Cocktail: Old Fashioned (pg. 134)

MAPLE-GLAZED QUAIL
VIC & ANTHONY'S STEAKHOUSE

Vic & Anthony's is definitely one of my favorite steakhouses in Houston. My visits always include a filet and a crab cake, which in my opinion, is the best in the city (crab cake recipe is in my Houston Classic Seafood cookbook). I dream about their au gratin potatoes regularly and cannot sleep through the night if I happen to have any leftovers in my refrigerator.

Recipe Notes: Semi-boneless quail are best for this dish. Quail may be procured frozen at most grocery stores and fresh at many farmer's markets.

YIELD: 6 SERVINGS

DRY RUB

½ cup	granulated sugar
1 Tbsp	kosher salt
½ tsp	dried oregano
½ Tbsp	cayenne pepper
1 Tbsp	paprika
½ Tbsp	granulated garlic
½ tsp	onion powder
⅛ tsp	black pepper

MAPLE GLAZE

2 Tbsp	pure maple syrup
2 Tbsp	chipotle peppers in adobo, puréed
1 Tbsp	Tabasco sauce
1 Tbsp	red wine vinegar
½ cup	unsalted butter, cubed

QUAIL

12	quail, semi-boneless
2 qt	canola oil, *to fry*
1 Tbsp	canola oil, divided, *to oven-fry*
	salad greens, lightly dressed
	Sriracha Hot Chili Sauce, *for garnish*

For the dry rub:

Combine all of the ingredients in a bowl and whisk until well combined.

For the maple glaze:

Heat all of the ingredients except for butter in a saucepot over medium heat. Once simmering, purée in butter using an immersion blender. Make sure the sauce doesn't boil. Sauce can be chilled and reheated by whisking into a scant amount of simmering water.

For the quail:

Cut the quail down the middle into 2 pieces. Place all of the quail pieces in a large mixing bowl. Add the dry rub and toss until well coated.

To fry: Preheat the deep-fryer to 350˚F. Add the quail and fry until crispy and just cooked through, about 2 to 3 minutes.

To oven-fry: Preheat the oven to 375˚F. Heat a large skillet over high heat. Add ½ tablespoon of oil. Add half the quail and sear, without moving, until the undersides are golden brown, about 2 to 3 minutes. Turn the quail and sear other side, about 2 to 3 minutes more. Transfer the quail to a rack on a sheet pan. Repeat with the remaining oil and quail. Transfer the sheet pan to the oven and roast until the quail is no longer pink and juices run clear, 8 to 10 minutes. Transfer the quail to a bowl and let stand 5 minutes.

Allow the quail to cool slightly, then toss with the maple glaze to thoroughly coat.

To serve:

Arrange the quail over lightly dressed salad greens. Garnish with several drops of Sriracha sauce.

Wine:	A Riesling
Beer:	A wheat beer, like Karbach Weisse Versa Wheat
Cocktail:	Jersey Mule (pg. 128)

PAN BORRACHO
MAX'S WINE DIVE

A savory bread pudding in every sense of the word, Pan Borracho (also known as drunken bread) is a customer favorite at MAX's Wine Dive. Equal parts smooth, gooey and comforting, it's the perfect dish to share as an appetizer or to soak up some of the party from the night before.

Recipe Notes: This is a great way to use bread that has seen fresher days, and it could also be a fun substitute for stuffing at Thanksgiving. Chef Michael Pellegrino uses Chablis wine in this recipe.

YIELD: 6 SERVINGS

Preheat the oven to 350°F.

For the cheese mixture:

In a small bowl, combine the provolone, Gruyère and Parmigiano-Reggiano and mix well.

For the wine mixture:

In a medium bowl, combine the white wine, cream, chicken stock, eggs and thyme. Whisk well.

In a large bowl, with your hands, rip the baguette into approximately ½-inch pieces.

Pour the wine mixture, half of the cheese mixture and the prosciutto in the bowl with the baguette. Mix well and let sit for 15 minutes.

Place the pan borracho mix in an oven-safe casserole dish or smaller, individual ramekins. Top with the remaining cheese mixture. Bake for about 25 minutes or until golden brown.

CHEESE MIXTURE
4 oz	provolone cheese, grated
4 oz	Gruyère cheese, grated
4 oz	Parmigiano-Reggiano cheese, grated

WINE MIXTURE
1 cup	white wine
1 cup	heavy cream
1 cup	chicken stock
5	eggs
1 Tbsp	fresh thyme, chopped
1	baguette (20-inch)
6 oz	prosciutto, chopped

Wine: A dry Sauvignon Blanc; a Pinot Noir or a Bordeaux-style blend; a brut Champagne
Beer: A Belgian witbier, like Estrella Damm Inedit
Cocktail: Summer Collins (pg. 139)

PISTACHIO-CRUSTED GOAT CHEESE CAKES
BENJY'S

These savory goat cheese cakes have been a customer favorite for years. They are especially great made with local or Texas-produced goat cheese. Check out offerings from Pola Artisan Cheese at Urban Harvest Farmers Markets (www.urbanharvest.org) or at Houston Dairymaids on Airline Drive or online at www. houstondairymaids.com.

Recipe Notes: Be sure to use raw pistachios when making the crust. Cakes should be thicker (rather than thinner) so they won't completely melt when cooking.

GOAT CHEESE CAKES

½ cup	fresh corn, off the cob
½ Tbsp	garlic, minced
½ Tbsp	olive oil
1 lb	goat cheese, softened
2 oz	cream cheese, softened
¼ cup	sun-dried tomatoes, chopped
2 Tbsp	fresh parsley, chopped
to taste	salt and pepper

MUSTARD RAISIN CHUTNEY

½	bay leaf
½ cup	rice vinegar
¾ cup	granulated sugar
½ cup	water
2 Tbsp	mustard seeds, toasted
½ cup	golden raisins
½	jalapeño

PISTACHIO CRUST

½ cup	raw pistachios, coarsely ground
1 cup	Panko bread crumbs, ground
½ Tbsp	olive oil
	bagel chips

YIELD: 12 GOAT CHEESE CAKES

For the goat cheese cakes:

Sauté the corn and garlic in the olive oil until corn is cooked, but not brown. Allow to cool. When cool, combine all of the cheese cake ingredients in a mixer. Mix well and season with salt and pepper. Refrigerate the mixture for at least 4 hours.

For the mustard raisin chutney:

Add the bay leaf, vinegar, sugar and water to a stockpot and bring to a boil. Reduce the heat to medium and add the mustard seeds, raisin and jalapeño. Cook for 15 minutes or until the raisins become rehydrated. Remove and discard the jalapeño and the bay leaf. Take half of the raisin mixture and purée in a blender until smooth. Add the puréed mix back into the raisin mix, then refrigerate until ready to serve.

For the pistachio crust:

In a shallow dish, mix the pistachios and Panko together. To shape the goat cheese cakes, use 2 heaping tablespoons and place the goat cheese balls in the pistachio and Panko mixture. Coat evenly and shape with a ring mold or round cookie cutter. Refrigerate the cakes again for a few hours.

To serve:

Add a little olive oil to a non-stick pan over medium-high heat. Once the pan is heated, add the goat cheese cakes and cook until golden brown, just about 2 minutes or so per side. Serve with the mustard raisin chutney and bagel chips.

Wine:	A Sauvignon Blanc
Beer:	A pale ale, like Karbach Hopadillo IPA
Cocktail:	Lemon Basil Gimlet (pg. 121)

SPICY HOUSE CRACKER JACKS
DOWN HOUSE

Although I have some faint Jiffy Pop stovetop-memories, for the last thirty years, I have made pre-packaged bagged popcorn in the microwave. I received a darling boxed Christmas card last year from Kristi, John and Sinclair Schiller, which included a bag of corn kernels and recipes. I have been a popcorn-making freak ever since. Come to find out, popcorn is chock-full of antioxidants in addition to being one hundred percent whole grain, high in fiber and low in calories (sans toppings). In fact, a single serving of popcorn has twice as many polyphenols as a piece of fruit.

I was thrilled when I saw this dish on the menu at Down House – who doesn't love Cracker Jacks? I must tell you, a glass of light, slightly sparkling Vinho Verde or a refreshing, cold beer and spicy popcorn and nuts are an excellent pairing!

Recipe Notes: This is SPICY stuff – probably not suitable for most children. In my opinion, the easiest way to pop corn kernels is in the microwave, in a brown paper bag or in a bowl covered with a plate (microwave-safe, of course) – two to three minutes is all it takes, and no oil is necessary. Matouk's Flambeau Sauce can be found at Fiesta stores in the international aisle, but Sambal or Sriracha Hot Chili Sauce may be substituted.

YIELD: 6 SERVINGS

For the popcorn:

Preheat the oven to 250°F. In a small saucepan over medium heat, combine the butter, brown sugar, soy sauce, honey and Matouk's Sauce. Boil for 5 minutes. Remove from heat; stir in baking soda. Stir well – it should become foam-like. Pour over your popped corn. Stir to coat well. Bake on a silicone mat or parchment paper-lined baking sheet for 45 minutes to 1 hour, stirring every 15 minutes. Allow it to cool at room temperature, and break up any clusters.

For the nuts:

Preheat oven to 300°F. In a small bowl, mix the sugars, salt and cayenne, making sure there are no lumps; set aside.

Beat the egg white, water and Matouk's sauce until frothy but not stiff. Add the almonds, and stir to coat evenly. Sprinkle nuts with sugar mixture, and toss until evenly coated. Spread sugared nuts in a single layer on baking sheet lined with parchment paper. Bake for 30 minutes, stirring occasionally. Remove from oven, and separate nuts as they cool. When completely cool, pour the nuts into a bowl, breaking up any that stick together.

To serve:

Combine the cooled popcorn and nuts and enjoy.

POPCORN

¼ cup	unsalted butter
½ cup	dark brown sugar
¼ tsp	soy sauce
2 Tbsp	honey
1 Tbsp	Matouk's Flambeau Sauce
¼ tsp	baking soda
2 qt	popcorn, popped

NUTS

1½ Tbsp	dark brown sugar
2½ Tbsp	granulated sugar
⅓ tsp	salt
⅛ tsp	cayenne pepper
¼ lb	raw almonds
½ Tbsp	egg white, room temperature
½ Tbsp	water
½ Tbsp	Matouk's Flambeau Sauce

Wine: A light, crisp Vinho Verde, like Santola
Beer: A blonde or Belgian ale, like Deep Ellum Farmhouse Wit, Southern Star Bombshell Blonde, or Ommegang Hennepin
Cocktail: Rusty Cross (pg. 122) or El Diablo (pg. 130)

CATAPLANA MUSSELS
PLONK!

Plonk Executive Chef Erin Smith cut her culinary teeth at Thomas Keller's Per Se in New York City, Mario Batali's Italian Wine Merchant and Batali's Babbo before eventually landing back in her hometown of Houston.

Cataplanas are a Portuguese cookware traditionally made of copper and shaped like two clamshells hinged at one end and able to be sealed using a clamp on either side. The shape and structure of the cataplana allows its liquid contents to create steam, cooking its solid contents. Shellfish is the most common food prepared in a cataplana, but you can also prepare other things like fish, meat, chicken, and vegetables. Don't have a cataplana? No worries – a stockpot and lid or a Dutch oven may be used in its place.

Recipe Notes: Chef Smith prefers Prince Edward Island (PEI) mussels. It's very important to store mussels on ice and in a container where oxygen is allowed to flow freely. If the mussels' shells are open and don't react by closing when you squeeze them, then discard – they are dead. To debeard the mussels, pull the stringy clumps from the shells while running under cold water. Make sure to rinse off any sand or dirt as well.

COCONUT CURRY SAUCE

¼ cup	red onion, large dice
I cup	green onions, white ends only
¾ cup	fresh ginger, peeled and thinly sliced
1½ Tbsp	garlic, minced
I cup	white wine (Riesling)
20 oz	coconut milk (1½ cans)
¼ cup	yellow curry paste
2 Tbsp	granulated sugar
¼ cup	olive oil

MUSSELS

3 Tbsp	garlic, minced
2 lb	mussels, debearded and cleaned
6	kaffir lime leaves
	chopped cilantro, *for garnish*

YIELD: 6 SERVINGS

For the coconut curry sauce:

Sauté the red onions, green onions, and ginger in olive oil over medium-low heat, until the onions are translucent, about 10 minutes. Add the garlic and sauté lightly for a few minutes, being careful not to brown or burn the garlic. Increase the heat to medium-high and deglaze with the white wine, allowing it to reduce by half. Add the coconut milk, yellow curry paste and sugar. Bring to a boil, then lower the heat to medium and simmer for 20 minutes. Check the seasoning and remove from heat. Using an immersion blender, purée the mixture, then strain through a fine-mesh sieve. The sauce may be stored in the refrigerator for 5 days or in the freezer for up to 2 months.

For the mussels:

Preheat the oven to 400˚F.

Spread the minced garlic on the bottom of a cataplana or a stockpot with a lid. Add the mussels, the kaffir lime leaves and the coconut curry sauce; mix well. Close the cataplana or put the lid on the stockpot and place in the oven. Cook for 15 minutes or until the mussels open.

To serve:

Garnish with chopped cilantro and serve immediately.

Wine:	A Pinot Blanc; a Pinot Noir; or a Champagne, such as Perrier-Jouët Belle Epoque
Beer:	An American pale lager, like Shiner Light Blonder or Mirror Pond Pale Ale
Cocktail:	Western Dreamer (pg. 128)

ASPARAGUS RICOTTA TARTS
MARK'S AMERICAN CUISINE

Although I have said it aloud many times, I'm certain it's never been printed.

Here it is: Mark Cox is my favorite chef in Houston. Believe it or not, I am a bit finicky about some foods, but if Mark Cox is cooking it, I'm eating it.

Recipe Notes: Pastry Chef Sam Major prefers to make his puff pastry from scratch, but frozen puff pastry sheets or shells work great for this recipe. You can also make a large tart instead of individual ones.

YIELD: 6 SERVINGS

For the puff pastry:

Roll out the puff pastry. Cut 6 pieces of puff pastry 4½- by 1¼-inch wide for the tart bases. Cut 12 strips ⅛- by 4½-inch wide and 12 strips ⅛- by 1-inch wide. Brush the bases lightly with the egg and adhere the thinner strips on the edges to form a border. Brush with a little more egg and dock the border with a fork. Reserve the remaining egg for the ricotta filling. Cover with plastic and refrigerate while you make the filling.

For the ricotta filling:

Preheat the oven to 400˚F.

Blanch the asparagus in boiling water until tender, 2 to 3 minutes, and then plunge into ice water to cool quickly. Drain and dry. Cut the tips of the asparagus off, about 1-inch and reserve for garnish.

Chop the stalks in a food processor and add the rest of the egg, the ricotta, salt, and olive oil. Process until smooth. Scrape the filling into a bowl and fold in the salami, Gruyère, mozzarella, and half of the Parmesan.

Spread the filling onto the puff pastry. Garnish with the asparagus tips and the remaining Parmesan.

Bake for 20 minutes or until bottom of the puff pastry is deep golden brown.

For the papaya slaw:

Combine the papaya, red and yellow tomatoes and jalapeño in a medium bowl.

In a small bowl, mix white wine, lime juice, oil and herbs. Add salt to taste.

Pour the dressing over the papaya, tomatoes, and jalapeños and toss to coat.

To serve:

Spoon the papaya slaw on top of the tarts. Garnish with toasted salami chips, if desired.

PUFF PASTRY
2	puff pastry sheets
1	egg, beaten

RICOTTA FILLING
½ lb	asparagus, cleaned
¼ cup	ricotta cheese
	egg, reserved from puff pastry
⅛ tsp	salt
3 Tbsp	Gruyère cheese, grated
2 Tbsp	mozzarella cheese, grated
2 tsp	Parmesan cheese, grated
2 tsp	olive oil
¼ cup	Genoa salami, finely chopped

PAPAYA SLAW
½ cup	green papaya, cut into thin strips
½ cup	red and yellow cherry tomatoes, halved
1	jalapeño, thinly sliced
1 Tbsp	white wine
1 Tbsp	fresh lime juice
1 Tbsp	cilantro, finely chopped
1 Tbsp	basil, chiffonade
2 Tbsp	olive oil
to taste	salt
	toasted salami chips, *for garnish*

Wine:	A Gewürztraminer
Beer:	A lager, like Shiner Ruby Redbird
Cocktail:	Mezcal Buck (pg. 132)

LAMB LOLLIPOPS
CRÚ FOOD & WINE BAR

Combined with the wonderful flavors of goat cheese, figs, balsamic vinegar and prosciutto, the lamb lollipops have been a staple at CRÚ Food & Wine Bar for several years.

Recipe Notes: It's important to know that New Zealand lamb is leaner than Australian and most domestic-raised lamb. Domestic lamb is a little less gamey, however. Pork chops or steak medallions can be substituted for the lamb chops. For the veal demi-glace, you can buy veal stock and reduce it to make demi-glace or buy demi-glace-paste at Spec's, HEB's Central Market and Kroger stores.

YIELD: 12 LAMB LOLLIPOPS

BALSAMIC REDUCTION

½ cup   balsamic vinegar
½ cup   honey

LAMB LOLLIPOPS

12   lamb chops
to taste   salt and pepper

FIG DEMI-GLACE

¼ cup   black fig jam
¾ cup   veal demi-glace

2 oz   prosciutto, crispy
1 Tbsp   fresh mint, chopped
2 oz   goat cheese, crumbled

For the balsamic reduction:

In a small saucepan over medium-low heat, combine the vinegar and the honey. Cook until reduced by half and set aside.

For the lamb lollipops:

Preheat the oven to 350˚F.

Season the lamb with salt and pepper, to taste. Heat a cast iron skillet over high heat and sear the lamb chops for 1½ minutes per side. Remove the lamb chops from the skillet and transfer to a rack on a half sheet pan. Cook in the oven to medium rare, about 7 minutes, or 130˚F. Cover loosely with foil.

For the fig demi-glace:

In the same skillet used to sear the lamb, combine the fig jam and the demi-glace over medium heat until lightly thickened, about 7 to 9 minutes.

To serve:

Spoon the warm fig demi-glace on the bottom of desired plate(s). Arrange the hot lamb lollipops on top.

Garnish with a drizzle of the balsamic reduction, then add the crispy prosciutto, mint and the goat cheese.

Wine: A Cabernet Sauvignon
Beer: A Belgian sour ale, like Monk's Cafe Flemish Sour Ale
Cocktail: Manhattan (pg. 124)

CRAB CAKE SLIDERS
TRULUCK'S

Truluck's has been a seafood institution in Houston for more than twenty years. While many guests prefer to experience their meals in traditional table-side fashion, Truluck's has developed a cult following for guests who prefer to indulge in cocktails and bites at the bar. These sliders are enough to satisfy your happy-hour guests while still allowing room for an entrée that may follow.

Recipe Note: Smoked olive oil can be found at HEB's Central Market or gourmet specialty stores, but regular olive oil may be substituted.

YIELD: 18 SLIDERS

For the crab cakes:

In a large mixing bowl, mix the mayonnaise with the fresh dill. Add the Dijon mustard, Old Bay, cayenne and salt. Gently fold in the crab meat. Add the saltines and allow to rest for 10 minutes. Scoop out ¼ cup portions and place on a pan lined with parchment paper. Free-form the crab cakes – don't roll the crab cakes into balls or cylinders. Melt a teaspoon of butter to a large skillet over medium-high heat and cook the crab cakes in batches, for about 2 minutes per side. Repeat with remaining butter and crab cakes.

For the avocado salad:

Halve the avocado and remove the pit. Cut each avocado half into 9 pieces. In a small bowl, combine the lemon juice, olive oil, shallots and Crystal hot sauce; mix well. Fold the avocado into the dressing carefully as to preserve the large chunks. Do not over mix and make guacamole. Add salt, to taste.

To serve:

Spread ½ tablespoon of avocado salad on the bottom buns and a tablespoon of tartar sauce on the top buns. Then add the crab cakes, top with ¼ piece of bacon and add the top buns. Push the bamboo picks through the olive halves and through the center of the sliders to secure.

CRAB CAKES

½ cup	mayonnaise
1 Tbsp	fresh dill, chopped
2 tsp	Grey Poupon Dijon mustard
2 tsp	Old Bay seasoning
½ tsp	cayenne pepper
1 tsp	sea salt
1 lb	premium blue crab claw meat
9	saltine crackers, crushed
1 Tbsp	clarified butter

AVOCADO SALAD

1	avocado
1 Tbsp	fresh lemon juice
2 Tbsp	shallot, minced
½ Tbsp	smoked olive oil
1 tsp	Crystal hot sauce
to taste	sea salt
6	applewood smoked bacon strips, cooked
1⅛ cups	tartar sauce
18	Hawaiian rolls, buttered and toasted
18	bamboo picks
9	pimento-stuffed green olives, halved

Wine:	A Riesling
Beer:	A Belgian lager, like Stella Artois
Cocktail:	Lemon Hat (pg. 129)

DUCK CONFIT TOSTADAS
KILLEN'S STEAKHOUSE

DUCK CONFIT

4	duck legs
to taste	salt and pepper
1 Tbsp	canola oil
1 qt	duck fat (traditional)
3	garlic cloves, crushed
3	fresh thyme sprigs
1	cinnamon stick
1 tsp	black peppercorns
1	star anise piece
1 tsp	juniper berries
2	bay leaves

BLUEBERRY PICO DE GALLO

1 tsp	olive oil
2 cups	fresh blueberries
1 Tbsp	granulated sugar
½ cup	yellow onion, finely diced
3	garlic cloves, minced
2 Tbsp	cilantro, chopped
2 Tbsp	jalapeño, finely diced
1 Tbsp	lime juice
to taste	salt and pepper

TOSTADAS

9	corn tortillas
	oil, *to fry*
	oil or cooking spray, *to oven-fry*
	micro-cilantro, *for garnish*
	thinly sliced radish, *for garnish*

Chef Ronnie Killen served these duck confit tostadas at the James Beard House in December 2011. This is a very colorful dish with a lot of flavor – it is ideal for summer when blueberries are in their prime and very sweet. Want to make these when blueberries aren't at their best? Use frozen blueberries instead.

Recipe Notes: Traditional duck confit is made by submerging the duck in duck fat and slow roasting. This was done long ago to help preserve the cooked duck. It's a delicious way to prepare the duck but a lighter (and less expensive) preparation technique follows.

YIELD: 6 SERVINGS

For the duck confit:

Preheat the oven to 225˚F. Season the duck legs with salt and pepper.

Traditional: In a sauté pan, heat the oil over medium-high heat and sear the duck legs on both sides, about 5 minutes. Place the duck legs in a 4-inch deep pan, add the duck fat and the remaining ingredients. Cover the pan with foil. Place in the oven to cook for 2 hours. Allow to cool for a few minutes, then debone and shred the meat with a fork. Discard the aromatics and reserve the duck fat for another use.

Lighter: Heat the canola oil in a sauté pan or cast iron skillet over medium-high heat. Place the duck legs in the pan, skin-side down and cook for 10 to 15 minutes, or until enough fat renders and the duck easily releases from pan. Flip the duck over and add all of the aromatics. Cover the pan with foil. Place in the oven and cook for 2 hours. Let rest for a few minutes, then debone and shred the meat with a fork.

For the blueberry pico de gallo:

Heat the oil in a sauté pan over medium heat, add the blueberries and the sugar. Cook for about 2 minutes or until the sugar is fully dissolved and the blueberries have released some of their juice; set aside to cool. In a medium-sized bowl, combine the yellow onion, garlic, cilantro, jalapeño, lime juice and blueberries; gently mix. Add salt and pepper to taste.

For the tostadas:

Use a cookie cutter to make round tostadas or simply cut the tortillas in half.

To fry: Heat 1-inch of canola oil in a large frying pan over medium-high heat to 350˚F. Fry a few chips at a time, turning occasionally with a slotted spoon, until crisp and lightly browned, about 1 minute or less. Drain the chips on a paper towel-lined plate and sprinkle lightly with salt.

To oven-fry: Preheat the oven to 350˚F. Place the tortillas on a baking sheet and spritz with olive oil or cooking spray. Bake for 7 to 10 minutes, then flip the tortillas over and cook for approximately 5 more minutes or until crispy. Remove from oven and sprinkle with salt.

To serve:

Arrange the tostadas on a serving dish, add the duck confit and top with a spoonful of blueberry pico de gallo. Garnish with micro-cilantro and radish slices.

Wine:	A northeastern Spanish Grenache
Beer:	A lambic, like Kriek Cherry Lambic
Cocktail:	Southern Hospitality (pg. 121) or Aviation (pg. 128)

UCHI SALAD
UCHI

Uchi's take on chips and salsa – their Uchi Salad – is a great way to get your greens on!

Recipe Notes: Kombu sheets (dried seaweed) may be found at HEB's Central Market, Whole Foods and at Asian markets. Kombu contains a high concentration of free glutamate, which imparts the flavor "umami," the famous savory fifth taste in Japanese cuisine. Togarashi is a seven-spice mixture and may be found at Asian markets or online.

YIELD: 6 SERVINGS

For the sushi zu:

Use a damp towel to remove the sediment from the Kombu. Combine the vinegar and sugar in a small saucepan and heat over low, until the sugar has dissolved. Remove from the heat and let cool to room temperature. Add the Kombu and steep for 10 minutes. Remove the Kombu and refrigerate until ready to use.

For the edamame-jalapeño dressing:

Roast 2 of the jalapeños under the broiler to char the skin, then peel and seed. Rough chop the garlic, shallots, and the fresh jalapeño. In a skillet over medium-low heat, sweat the edamame, garlic and shallots until translucent, about 8 to 10 minutes, then strain and reserve the oil. In a blender, add the edamame mixture, the roasted jalapeños, and the fresh jalapeño. Add the water and purée until smooth. Add the sushi zu and the remaining oil through the top of the blender and process to emulsify. The consistency should be that of mayonnaise.

For the yellow bell pepper piperade:

In a skillet over medium-low heat, sweat the pepper, shallot and garlic in the olive oil until tender, about 5 minutes. Season with salt and paprika, remove from heat. Refrigerate until cool, then add the parsley. Reserve at room temperature until ready to use.

For the Panko rice:

Preheat the oven to 325˚F. Spread the Panko on a parchment paper-lined sheet pan. Toast until golden, about 7 minutes; let cool. Fry the rice in a small amount of oil at 350˚F for 1 to 2 minutes, or spritz the rice with cooking spray and bake at 350˚F for about 10 minutes, until crisp, then break up by hand. Combine the Panko and rice in a high-powered blender, season with togarashi and salt and pulse until combined.

To serve:

Squeeze a small amount of lemon juice and sprinkle a little sea salt onto the baby romaine leaves; drizzle with olive oil. Place an equal amount of baby romaine leaves into shot glasses, stem-side down. Sprinkle with the Panko rice. Partially fill a cup or bowl with the edamame-jalapeño dressing. Spoon a little of the room temperature yellow bell pepper piperade on top of the dressing to finish.

Wine:	An Austrian Grüner Veltliner
Beer:	A Belgian wheat ale, like Blanche de Bruxelles
Cocktail:	Momotsuki (pg. 139)

SUSHI ZU

1 oz	Kombu
½ cup	rice vinegar
½ cup	granulated sugar

EDAMAME-JALAPEÑO DRESSING

2½	fresh jalapeños
2 cups	shelled edamame
⅔ cup	garlic, rough chop
⅓ cup	shallot, rough chop
⅓ cup	vegetable oil
⅓ cup	sushi zu
½ cup	water
2 tsp	kosher salt

YELLOW BELL PEPPER PIPERADE

1 cup	yellow bell pepper, brunoise
⅓ cup	shallot, brunoise
2 Tbsp	garlic, brunoise
¼ cup	olive oil
⅛ tsp	kosher salt
¾ tsp	paprika
1⅓ Tbsp	parsley leaves, finely chopped

PANKO RICE

¾ cup	Panko bread crumbs
2 Tbsp	rice, cooked
pinch	togarashi
pinch	salt
½ cup	oil, to fry
	cooking spray, to bake

40 oz	baby romaine leaves
drizzle	fresh lemon juice
to taste	sea salt
drizzle	olive oil

CHIPOTLE CHICKEN SOPES
JULIA'S BISTRO

This is a traditional dish from Culiacán, Mexico. Co-owner Ric Ancira was introduced to sopes as a young boy. He would often ask for something to eat while dinner was being prepared. A small sope would be made on the spot using the mass for the fresh corn tortillas, the meat stewing for dinner and the garniture as the condiments.

YIELD: 6 SERVINGS

SOPES

2 cups	masa (instant corn flour)
1½ cups	hot water
½ tsp	salt

CHICKEN FRICASSEE

1 lb	boneless chicken breast
6	small tomatoes
2 Tbsp	onions, chopped
¼ tsp	salt
¼ tsp	black pepper
1 Tbsp	chipotle peppers in adobo, puréed
1 Tbsp	vegetable oil
½ cup	purple cabbage, julienned
½ cup	queso fresco, crumbled
	cilantro, *garnish*
	lime wedges, *for garnish*

For the sopes:

Heat a cast iron skillet or sauté pan over medium-high heat. In a medium bowl, combine the masa, salt and hot water. Mix to form a dough. Separate into 18 ping-pong ball sized balls. Using a tortilla press or a plate, flatten to make small sopes (about 3-inches diameter). Cook for 3 minutes per side. After cooking, pinch around 1 side of the entire perimeter of each sope. Set aside.

For the chicken fricassee:

Bring a pot of water to a boil, add the chicken and reduce the heat to a simmer. Cover and let cook 15 minutes. Remove from the heat, cool, then shred the chicken.

In a separate saucepot, put the tomatoes on to boil for 10 minutes. Strain the water, then purée the tomatoes in a blender. Heat the oil in a sauce pan over medium-high heat, add the onions, salt, tomato purée and the puréed chipotle. Bring to a boil and then add the shredded chicken to the sauce. Remove from heat.

To serve:

Preheat the oven to 375˚F. Place the sopes on a baking sheet and into the oven for 5 to 10 minutes. Remove from the oven and top each sope with the chicken fricassee. Top with cabbage and queso fresco. Garnish with cilantro leaves and lime wedges.

Wine:	A Malbec
Beer:	A Mexican lager, like Corona
Cocktail:	Flamingo (pg. 127)

BALSAMIC FIG CROSTINI
QUATTRO, FOUR SEASONS HOTEL

Figs are as much a part of Italian history as Pompeii or the Appian Way (their popularity evident by the number of ancient emperors done in by poison-laced figs). They are eaten at all times of the day, but especially during the popular Italian Apéritivo, a preprandial time of relaxation, cocktails and nibbles.

Vinoteca, the casual dining spot and wine bar next door to Quattro, hosts its own Apéritivo with an ever-changing menu of Executive Chef Maurizio Ferrarese's creations. For this favorite, he uses fresh, fleshy figs, just ripe enough to stay firm after being warmed in a reduced balsamic and local honey glaze. Using locally produced honey or honey that specifies the types of flowers from which the bees gathered pollen can enhance the flavors in different ways. Be sure to always use the very best olive oil you can afford!

YIELD: 18 PIECES

For the orange-basil segments:

In a small bowl, combine the orange segments with the basil and drizzle with olive oil.

For the balsamic-glazed figs:

Place the balsamic and honey in a sauce pan over medium heat. Reduce by half; stirring occasionally, about 10 to 15 minutes. Add the figs and cook for approximately 8 to 10 minutes, until the balsamic is reduced to a glaze and the figs are nicely coated.

For the crostini:

Spray or brush the baguette slices with olive oil and toast in the oven at 300°F, until lightly browned, about 5 minutes per side. Remove from the oven.

To serve:

Spread a heaping teaspoon of mascarpone cheese on the crostini and top with 2 pieces of balsamic-glazed figs and an orange-basil segment. Garnish each crostini with micro-basil or basil chiffonade.

To segment an orange:

Cut off the top and bottom of the orange. Following the curve of the orange, trim away the skin on all sides. Slide your knife between the membrane and each segment until you reach the middle of the orange; repeat on the other side of the segment. Pop the segment out and continue with the rest of the orange.

ORANGE-BASIL SEGMENTS
1	orange
5	basil leaves, chiffonade
1 tsp	olive oil

BALSAMIC-GLAZED FIGS
½ cup	balsamic vinegar
¼ cup	honey
9	figs, halved

CROSTINI
1	baguette, sliced
spritz	olive oil
½ cup	mascarpone cheese
	micro-basil or herbs, *for garnish*

Wine: A Champagne, such as Chandon California Extra Dry Riche
Beer: A wheat beer, like Southern Star Bombshell Blonde
Cocktail: The Ambassador (pg. 134)

CURRY CHICKEN SALAD
MKT BAR, PHOENICIA SPECIALTY FOODS

Houston's family-owned Phoenicia Specialty Foods offers more than fifteen thousand gourmet international foods from more than fifty countries. Their west Houston and downtown locations offer fresh produce, a vast selection of spices and a smorgasbord of prepared foods, including some of the best baklava and pita bread in town. They also have a nice assortment of kitchen tools, cookware and accessories available.

Enjoy live music, gastro-pub fare, wine and beer at their industrial chic MKT BAR (downtown location).

CHICKEN BREASTS

½ tsp	white vinegar
1 tsp	lemon juice
1 tsp	fresh garlic, minced
2 Tbsp	fresh parsley, chopped
⅓ tsp	white pepper, ground
2 Tbsp	vegetable oil
1½ lb	chicken breast tenders

CHICKEN SALAD

1⅛ cups	celery, small dice
⅓ cup	red bell pepper, small dice
⅓ cup	red onion, small dice
¾ cup	dried cherries, pitted
2 Tbsp	cilantro leaves, chopped
½ cup	walnut halves, toasted
1½ cups	mayonnaise
½ Tbsp	curry powder
½ Tbsp	ground turmeric
2 Tbsp	granulated sugar
1½ tsp	kosher salt
½ tsp	ground black pepper
	pita chips or bread, quartered and lightly toasted
	chopped fresh parsley, *for garnish*

YIELD: 6 SERVINGS

For the chicken breasts:

In a shallow container, combine the first 6 ingredients (vinegar through vegetable oil) and mix well. Add the chicken and marinate, refrigerated, for 1 to 2 hours.

Preheat the oven to 375°F.

Place the chicken on a sheet pan and bake for 17 minutes. Remove from oven and let cool. Cut into 1-inch cubes.

For the chicken salad:

In a large mixing bowl, combine the chicken breasts, celery, peppers, onions, cherries, cilantro and walnuts.

In a smaller bowl, combine the mayonnaise, curry powder, turmeric, sugar, salt and pepper and mix until evenly blended. Using a rubber spatula, fold the mayonnaise mixture into the chicken mixture. Fold together until the chicken mixture is evenly coated.

To serve:

Spoon the chicken salad into a large serving bowl and surround with pita chips or toasted pita bread. Garnish with chopped parsley.

Wine:	A Pinot Noir; or Prosecco
Beer:	A German wheat beer, like Weihenstephaner Hefeweissbier
Cocktail:	Sachin Tendulkar (pg. 124)

AHI TUNA TACOS
MONARCH, HOTEL ZAZA

The Terrace at Hotel ZaZa's Monarch offers gorgeous fountain and garden views. It's the perfect spot to enjoy a bite and glass of bubbly before or after a trip to the Museum of Fine Arts.

Recipe Notes: Sushi-grade tuna makes all the difference when making tuna tartar. Fresno peppers are red jalapeños. If you prefer things really spicy, add more Sriracha sauce. Wontons may be deep-fried or oven-baked into whatever shape you desire.

YIELD: 6 SERVINGS

For the wontons:

To fry: Heat the oil to 350˚F. Fry for 2 minutes or until golden brown.

To bake: Preheat the oven to 375˚F. Shape the wontons into tacos or tostadas, spritz with cooking spray and bake for 7 to 9 minutes.

For the tuna:

Dice the tuna and place in a steel bowl. Add the sesame seeds, sesame oil, salt, pepper and Sriracha sauce; mix well. Reserve in the refrigerator until needed.

For the cucumber slaw:

Combine the cucumber, Fresno pepper and red onion in a medium bowl. Add the rice wine vinegar, crushed red pepper and a teaspoon each of sesame oil, soy and fish sauce. Mix well and allow to marinate for at least 10 minutes.

To serve:

Fill the wonton shells or crisps with about 2 tablespoons of the tuna and top with cucumber slaw.

WONTONS

1 pack	wonton skins
	oil, *to fry*
	cooking spray or an oil mister, *to bake*

TUNA

1½ lb	Ahi tuna (sushi-grade)
1 Tbsp	black sesame seeds
1 Tbsp	sesame oil
¼ tsp	salt
¼ tsp	pepper
1 Tbsp	Sriracha Hot Chili Sauce

CUCUMBER SLAW

1	English cucumber, julienned
4	Fresno peppers, julienned
½ cup	red onion, julienned
2 Tbsp	rice wine vinegar
2 tsp	crushed red pepper
1 tsp	soy sauce
1 tsp	fish sauce
1 tsp	sesame oil

Wine:	An off-dry Vouvray
Beer:	A blonde ale, like Real Ale Brewing Co. Firemans #4
Cocktail:	Skinny Watermelon Margarita (pg. 130)

VEAL RAVIOLI
ARTURO'S UPTOWN ITALIANO

Veal Ravioli is just one of the sixteen raviolis offered as specials during Arturo's Annual Ravioli Festival each February. Other variations that are particularly popular during the festival include: artichoke, burrata cheese, lobster, lamb and owner Bill Sadler's favorite, good ol' Texas deer sausage. Your imagination is the only limit in regard to ravioli filling.

Recipe Notes: Use fresh or frozen pasta sheets to make six larger ravioli as pictured or wonton wrappers for twelve smaller ravioli. If black truffles are unavailable, a drizzle of truffle oil will suffice.

YIELD: 6 SERVINGS

For the veal:

In a large skillet, heat the olive oil over medium-high heat. Add the veal, garlic, onion and mushrooms. Cook for 5 minutes. Add the salt, pepper, oregano and brandy and stir to combine. Let cool and drain the juices.

For the cream cheese mixture:

In a medium bowl, combine the egg, cream cheese, Parmesan and Panko. Fold the cream cheese mixture into the veal.

Prepare a floured surface for the pasta squares or wonton wrappers. Set a small bowl with the egg or water nearby. Place a dollop of the filling mixture in the center of each square or wrapper, then brush the outside ½-inch of the wrapper with a little egg or water, and do the same to the wrapper you will place on top, moist sides facing each other. Align and press the top wrapper down on the bottom wrapper. Press around the outside edges with a fork. Use a pizza cutter to trim any uneven edges.

Bring the water to a boil in a deep sauté pan or stockpot. Add the olive oil. Drop in the ravioli, a few at a time, and cook for 2 to 3 minutes. The ravioli will float when they are done cooking.

For the lime beurre blanc sauce:

Cook the white wine and garlic in a small saucepan over medium heat for 3 to 4 minutes. Add the salt, butter, parsley and lime juice, stirring to combine. Reduce the heat to low and cook for 2 to 3 minutes.

To serve:

Pour the lime beurre blanc sauce over the ravioli. Garnish with shaved truffles and toasted walnuts.

VEAL

½ Tbsp	extra-virgin olive oil
½ lb	veal, chopped
2½ tsp	garlic, chopped
1⅓ Tbsp	red onion, diced
⅔ cup	mushrooms, finely chopped
⅓ tsp	salt
pinch	white pepper
⅛ tsp	dried oregano
½ Tbsp	Christian Brothers Brandy

CREAM CHEESE MIXTURE

2¼ tsp	egg, beaten
3 oz	cream cheese, softened
2 Tbsp	Parmesan cheese, grated
2½ Tbsp	Panko bread crumbs
2 Tbsp	egg, beaten or water
12	pasta squares or 24 wonton wrappers
2 qt	water
1 tsp	olive oil

LIME BEURRE BLANC SAUCE

⅓ cup	white wine
½ Tbsp	garlic, chopped
¼ tsp	salt
6 oz	unsalted butter
½ Tbsp	fresh parsley, chopped
½ Tbsp	fresh lime juice
3 oz	black truffles, shaved
½ cup	walnuts, toasted

Wine:	A dry Vouvray or a Cru Beaujolais
Beer:	A European pale lager, like Peroni
Cocktail:	Basilini (pg. 121)

TUSCAN CHICKEN SKEWERS
RISTORANTE CAVOUR, HOTEL GRANDUCA

Hotel Granduca's signature restaurant, the elegant Ristorante Cavour, was named for the first Prime Minister of Italy, Count Cavour.

Executive Chef Renato DePirro sources as many of his ingredients as possible from Italy. Although this sauce is Tuscan-born – made from Tuscan berries, herbs, oils and honey – it's been modified by adding just a bit of smokiness, to better suit Texans' tastes.

Chef DePirro proudly serves Piedmontese beef, which I have long been a fan of. Piedmontese cows carry a double inactive myostatin gene, which makes it one of the healthiest meats you can find. This will blow your mind – Piedmontese beef has fewer calories, fat and cholesterol than a chicken breast, and is loaded with omega-3 fatty acids.

Recipe Note: Marinate the chicken for different flavors like lemon, herbs or teriyaki sauce.

YIELD: 12 SKEWERS

For the chicken skewers:

Soak the bamboo skewers in water for an hour to keep from burning later.

Heat your grill to medium-high, or preheat your oven to 375˚F.

Rinse the chicken and cut it into 12 strips. Thread the chicken pieces onto the skewers. Season the chicken with olive oil, salt and pepper. Grill until done, about 4 minutes per side.

Or, arrange the skewers on a sheet pan. Bake in the oven, until just cooked through, about 8 minutes.

For the Tuscan barbecue sauce:

Finely chop the herbs. Place all of the ingredients into a blender. Blend until smooth and creamy.

To serve:

Place the mixed greens on the bottom of a serving plate, then top with the chicken skewers. Serve alongside a bowl of Tuscan barbecue sauce.

CHICKEN SKEWERS

12	bamboo skewers
2	boneless chicken breasts
1 Tbsp	olive oil
to taste	salt and pepper

TUSCAN BARBECUE SAUCE

1	rosemary sprig
1	thyme sprig
1	sage sprig
1 cup	fresh raspberries
½ cup	extra-virgin olive oil
¼ cup	red wine vinegar
1 tsp	liquid smoke
to taste	honey or agave nectar
to taste	salt and pepper
	mixed greens

Wine: A fruity Sauvignon Blanc
Beer: A pale ale, like Shiner Wild Hare Pale Ale
Cocktail: Breath of Fresh Pear (pg. 127)

DEVILED EGG FRIED OYSTERS
LIBERTY KITCHEN

Savannah-style fried oysters top the deviled eggs and are garnished with a little piece of crispy, smoked bacon. The combination of textures and flavors will blow your skirt up – at least it did mine! This is gourmet picnic food, folks!

Recipe Notes: Scared of the deep fryer? I also oven-fried the oysters to crisp perfection (instructions below). For a variation, add some minced serrano peppers to the egg yolk mixture.

YIELD: 16 PIECES

For the deviled eggs:

Fill a stockpot with cold water. Add the eggs and bring to a boil. Boil the eggs for 9 minutes; turn off the heat. Allow to rest for 3 minutes. Peel the eggs, then cut in half lengthwise. Separate the yolks and place in a bowl. Smash the yolks with a fork and fold in the mayonnaise, olive oil, pickles and mustard. Season to taste with salt and pepper. Add more mayonnaise if necessary (depending on the size of the yolks). Using a spoon or a piping bag, fill the egg halves with the yolk mixture. Garnish with a dash of smoked paprika and a sprinkle of freshly chopped parsley.

For the bacon:

Pan fry or microwave 4 to 6 slices of bacon to desired crispness. Cut the bacon into 1- to 2-inch pieces.

For the oysters:

Soak the oysters in buttermilk (this may be done for a few hours). In a bowl, combine the flour and seasonings. Remove the oysters from the buttermilk and shake off excess liquid. Dredge in the flour mixture.

To fry: Heat the oil in a deep skillet or fryer to 350˚F. Pan or deep fry for about 1 minute, depending on the size of the oyster, just until you see a bit of color on the flour. Remove and drain on a paper towel.

To oven-fry: Preheat the oven to 425˚F. Place the floured oysters on a rack on sheet pan. Spritz generously with cooking spray or olive oil. Bake for 10 minutes. Turn the oysters over, give them another spritz of cooking spray or oil and cook for 8 to 10 minutes.

To serve:

Top each deviled egg with an oyster and a piece of bacon.

DEVILED EGGS

8	eggs
2 Tbsp	mayonnaise
1 Tbsp	extra-virgin olive oil
2 tsp	pickles, chopped
1 tsp	mustard
to taste	kosher salt and pepper
dash	smoked paprika
½ Tbsp	parsley, chopped

BACON

4 to 6	smoked bacon slices

OYSTERS

16	oysters, shucked
¾ cup	buttermilk
¾ cup	all-purpose flour
1 tsp	smoked paprika
to taste	kosher salt and pepper
	canola oil, *to fry*
	cooking spray or oil, *to oven-fry*

Wine: A Chardonnay
Beer: A blonde ale, like Southern Star Bombshell Blonde
Cocktail: Norhill (pg. 126)

CHICKEN LETTUCE WRAPS
GIGI'S ASIAN BISTRO & DUMPLING BAR

Gigi's Asian Bistro & Dumpling Bar is a see-and-be-seen foodie paradise, beloved for its exotic ambiance and modern Asian cuisine. Gigi's father, James Huang, helped introduce Houstonians to Chinese cuisine when he debuted Hunan in 1976. The Post Oak location has since closed, but Gigi carries out the family name with a chic restaurant that features her own unique style and tastes.

Recipe Notes: Lettuce wraps are traditionally served in iceberg lettuce, but if you're looking for a little more nutritional punch, consider bibb, butter or romaine lettuce, or other leafy greens such as cabbage or kale. Another serving idea is to place the lettuce leaves on a platter and the chicken mixture in a bowl and allow people to make their own wraps.

YIELD: 6 SERVINGS

For the sauce:

In a small cup, dissolve the cornstarch in the water. Place all of the ingredients into a medium bowl and whisk together. Set aside.

For the chicken mixture:

Mince or finely chop the chicken breast. Add half of the oil to a large skillet over medium-high heat. Sauté the chicken for 4 to 5 minutes. Remove the chicken from the skillet with a slotted spoon and set aside to cool. Keep any remaining oil in the skillet and keep it hot.

Mince the water chestnuts and mushrooms to the size of small peas. Pour the remaining oil into the same skillet you used previously, keeping it over high heat. Add the garlic, scallions, water chestnuts and mushrooms and cook for 2 to 3 minutes. Add the chicken and stir to combine. Whisk the sauce and pour into the skillet while stirring continuously. Lower the heat to medium and cook for another 2 to 3 minutes. Remove from the heat and allow to cool slightly, about 5 minutes.

To serve:

Fill each lettuce leaf with about ½ cup of the chicken mixture. Serve with Sriracha sauce, and crushed peppers in oil.

SAUCE

1 tsp	cornstarch
1 tsp	water
¾ cup	soy sauce
1 cup	granulated sugar
2½ tsp	fresh ginger, minced
2 Tbsp	garlic, minced
¾ cup	white vinegar
2 tsp	white pepper
2 tsp	sesame oil
2 tsp	white cooking wine
1 tsp	sesame paste
3 Tbsp	crushed red pepper flakes

CHICKEN MIXTURE

1½ lb	boneless skinless chicken breasts
¼ cup	vegetable oil
1 Tbsp	garlic, minced
1 cup	water chestnuts
1 cup	mushrooms
½ cup	green scallions, chopped
12	iceberg lettuce leaves

Wine: An off-dry Riesling or a Pinot Gris
Beer: A malty brown ale, like Real Ale Brewhouse Brown Ale
Cocktail: Momotsuki (pg. 139)

CEVICHE
CONCEPCIÓN

Although it's considered Peru's national dish, there's an age old argument as to ceviche's origin – was it with the Incas in South America? The Incas are thought to have preserved their fish with fruit juice, salt and chiles. Or is its origin Arabian, brought to Peru by the Moorish immigrants (with limes from the Spanish conquistadors) and simply reinterpreted by the Peruvians?

Recipe Notes: Chef Jonathan Jones says for easier juicing, you should first soak the limes in warm water for twenty minutes. You can be as experimental as you like but always use the freshest fish available, and marinate or "cook" in lime or other citrus juices, chiles and herbs for at least an hour. Always remember, if raw fish smells fishy, it isn't fresh!

YIELD: 6 SERVINGS

CEVICHE

2 cups	fresh lime juice (about 16 limes)
1 lb	fresh fish fillets
¼ cup	sea salt

WATERMELON JUICE

1	small watermelon, seedless
1	habanero chile, minced
¼ cup	fresh lime juice
¼ tsp	sea salt
1	radish, thinly sliced
1	small red onion, julienned
1	fresh Mexican mint marigold or tarragon sprig
drizzle	extra-virgin olive oil

For the ceviche:

Juice all of the limes. Set aside.

Make sure all of the bones and blood line are removed from the fish. Sprinkle both sides of the fish with a generous amount of sea salt and allow to "cure" in the refrigerator for 10 minutes. Rinse off the salt and dry with a non-terrycloth towel.

Place the fish in a non-reactive pan (or a plastic bag) and completely submerge it in lime juice for up to an hour or until the outer flesh turns opaque.

For the watermelon juice:

Peel the watermelon and pulse the red flesh in a food processor or blender. Strain out and discard the pulp. Reserve the juice from the watermelon.

Add the habanero, lime juice and sea salt to 2 cups of watermelon juice. Add more or less of any of these ingredients to suit your taste, to create a slightly acidified and seasoned watermelon juice.

To serve:

When you're ready to serve, remove the fish from the lime juice and dry. Thinly slice the fish and place in a bowl with some of the red onion, radish and mint marigold or tarragon leaves. Add a small amount of the watermelon juice to the bowl. Season with salt, to taste.

Place the ceviche into 6 small, chilled bowls and add some more of the watermelon juice to each bowl. Drizzle with some extra-virgin olive oil and serve.

If you like more heat, add more chile to the watermelon juice or garnish with additional chile at the end.

Wine:	A Basque Txakoli rosé
Beer:	An IPA, like Bear Republic Racer 5
Cocktail:	Skinny Margarita (pg. 130)

Pastry Chef extraordinaire Rebecca Masson made Houstonians proud in her recent appearance on Top Chef Just Desserts. She's known around town as the "Sugar Hooker" and is famous for her fluffernutter cookies, aka baked crack (fluffernutter recipe is in my Houston Classic Desserts cookbook). Her delicious treats may be procured at Fluff Bake Bar in Revival Market on Heights Boulevard or ordered online at www.fluffbakebar.com.

Recipe Notes: Although you want to make sure you don't burn the butter too much, don't be too shy either, because the caramel flavor of toasted butter is the best part of the financiers. Chef Masson cooks hers until there are grains of burnt butter residue at the bottom of the pot. The granulated sugar in the poached plums may be replaced with ⅓ cup of agave nectar.

POACHED PLUMS

⅔ cup	white wine
⅔ cup	water
¾ cup	granulated sugar
2-inch	cinnamon stick
1-inch	vanilla bean
1	star anise piece
1 Tbsp	fresh ginger, crushed
1	clove
¼ tsp	orange zest
2	plums

FINANCIERS

1 cup	powdered sugar
¼ cup	all-purpose flour
½ cup	almond flour
⅓ cup	egg whites
⅓ cup	unsalted butter
¾ tsp	almond extract
¼ tsp	vanilla extract

YIELD: 24 FINANCIERS

For the poached plums:

Cut the plums in half and remove the pits. Cut each plum half into 6 pieces. Combine all of the ingredients (except the plums) in a small pot over high heat. Bring to a boil and then reduce to a very light simmer. Add the plums and cook for about 10 minutes. Don't overcook the plums or they will turn to mush. Remove from the heat and pour all into a container to cool.

For the financiers:

Preheat the oven to 375°F or the convection oven to 350°F.

In the bowl of a stand mixer fitted with the paddle attachment, add the powdered sugar, flour, almond flour and mix until combined. Add the egg whites and beat for about 4 minutes.

In a small saucepan, cook the butter over medium heat until the foam subsides and the butter smells of hazelnuts. Constantly stir the butter while it's cooking so the brown bits don't stick to the pot. Pour the butter *slowly* into the mixer (on low) until combined. Add the almond and vanilla extracts.

Spray a mini-muffin pan with cooking spray (or use a silicone muffin pans). Scoop the batter into the molds. Top each with a poached plum.

Bake for 25 to 30 minutes or until golden brown.

Wine:	Moscato d'Asti or a demi-sec Champagne
Beer:	A Belgian ale, like Trappistes Rochefort
Cocktail:	East Coast (pg. 135)

MAYELA'S COOKIES
BACKSTREET CAFÉ

At one of Pastry Chef Ruben Ortega's first jobs, he and a co-worker were asked to create a delicious, soft cookie. After many trials, they finally perfected these small chocolate cookies. An instant hit but nameless, Chef Ortega decided to name them after his co-worker.

Recipe Notes: Orange liqueur such as Grand Marnier, Cointreau or Controy work well in this recipe. I tested a much larger version of the recipe initially and stored the majority of the baked cookies in the freezer, mainly to get them out of my line of sight. Of course, I quickly discovered that they are equally delicious frozen!

YIELD: 24 COOKIES

In a double boiler, melt the chocolate and butter. Remove from the heat. Add the eggs, ½ cup of the sugar, the orange extract and liqueur. Whisk after each addition.

Sift together the flour and baking powder. Fold into the chocolate mixture, making sure to incorporate well. Sift together the almond flour and the salt. Fold into the chocolate mixture, making sure it's well combined.

Transfer the dough to a piece of plastic wrap and place in the freezer until cold and firm, about 30 to 45 minutes. This will make the dough much easier to handle.

Preheat oven to 350°F.

Divide the dough into 24 equal small rounds, about ½-inch in diameter. Roll each dough ball into the remaining sugar and then through the powdered sugar. Place the sugared dough balls on a sheet pan lined with parchment paper. Place in the oven and bake for 10 to 12 minutes. The cookies should have a soft interior.

6 oz	dark chocolate
2 Tbsp	unsalted butter
2	eggs
1 cup	granulated sugar, divided
¼ tsp	orange extract
2½ Tbsp	orange liqueur
5⅓ Tbsp	all-purpose flour
⅓ tsp	baking powder
½ cup	almond flour
⅛ tsp	salt
½ cup	powdered sugar

Wine: A Moscato d'Asti or a demi-sec Champagne
Beer: A stout, like Southern Star Buried Hatchet Stout
Cocktail: Brandy Milk Punch (pg. 141)

STRAWBERRY LAVENDER GELATO
TRENTINO GELATO

This flavor creation was developed by Trentino Gelato's Marcelo Kriendel and Top Chef Masters superstar Monica Pope of Sparrow Bar + Cookshop (formerly t'afia restaurant). Chef Pope was looking for an aromatic seasonal berry flavor – which is how the idea of lavender seeds came into play.

This is not the gelato maker's first collaboration with chefs – he has developed flavors with many chefs in Houston and Austin. Most of the chef-created offerings, along with other delicious flavors, are sold at HEB's Central Market stores, Whole Foods and Hubbell & Hudson, as well as many local restaurants.

Recipe Notes: Lavender seeds may be purchased at Central Market in the bulk food section or special ordered from Whole Foods. Be sure to use fresh, organic strawberries, if possible. Although strawberries are full of nutrients, they are also one of the most pesticide-harboring fruits, so if ever there was a time to go organic...

YIELD: 6 SERVINGS

1½ cups	heavy cream
1½ cups	whole milk
1 cup	granulated sugar
1 cup	fresh organic strawberries, puréed
1 tsp	lavender seeds

In a medium saucepan combine the cream, milk, and sugar.

Cook over medium heat, stirring until the sugar is dissolved, then cook until bubbles form around the edges of the pan.

Remove from the heat and add the strawberry purée and the lavender seeds. Stir and let stand for 30 minutes.

Cover and refrigerate for at least 2 hours, or until thoroughly chilled.

Remove the mix and transfer it to a gelato maker. Freeze according to the manufacturer's instructions.

Wine: A demi-sec Champagne, like Laurent-Perrier Demi-Sec
Beer: A pale lager, like Abita Strawberry Harvest Lager or Shiner Blonde
Cocktail: Aviation (pg. 128)

COCONUT CREAM TARTS
SULLIVAN'S STEAKHOUSE

Sullivan's Steakhouse is a 1940s Chicago-style restaurant and lounge. It's meant to be your total night out on the town, complete with dinner, live music and dancing (live music in their Ringside lounge Wednesday through Saturday).

Recipe Note: Mini springform pans may be found locally at Sur La Table.

YIELD: 4 SERVINGS

For the nilla wafer crust:

Put the vanilla wafers in a blender or food processor and pulse until you have crumbs.

Add the remaining ingredients and pulse until they come together. Spray the sides and bottom of the mini springform pans with cooking spray or coat with melted butter. Press the crumbs into the bottom and onto the sides of the pans.

For the coconut cream custard:

In a medium saucepot over medium-high heat, bring the whole milk, coconut milk, shredded coconut, ½ cup of the sugar and salt to a simmer. Stir frequently, for 3 to 4 minutes, until the sugar dissolves.

In a medium stainless steel bowl, combine the remaining 3 tablespoons of sugar, the egg yolks and cornstarch; whisk until smooth.

Using a whisk, slowly temper the egg yolk mixture with the heated milk mixture while constantly stirring. Once the egg mixture is tempered, add the remaining liquid, and whisk to combine. Transfer the mixture back to the saucepot and stir with a wire whisk until the mixture thickens and reaches a boil. Remove from the heat; whisk in the diced butter, a few pieces at a time, until well combined.

Distribute the custard evenly between the pans. Cover each with plastic wrap, allowing the plastic to touch the top of the custard (to prevent a film from forming). Refrigerate for at least 4 hours.

To serve:

Carefully remove the springform pans. Top each custard with 1 or 2 dollops of whipped cream. Garnish with a sprig of mint and toasted coconut.

NILLA WAFER CRUST

1¼ cups	vanilla wafers
2¼ tsp	granulated sugar
3⅓ Tbsp	unsalted butter, melted but cooled
1¼ Tbsp	unsweetened coconut, toasted

COCONUT CREAM CUSTARD

1 cup	whole milk
13 oz	coconut milk (1 can)
½ cup	coconut flake, unsweetened
⅔ cup	granulated sugar, divided
pinch	iodized salt
6 Tbsp	egg yolks
¼ cup	cornstarch
2 Tbsp	unsalted butter, ½-inch dice
¾ tsp	vanilla extract
2 cups	freshly whipped cream mint sprigs, *for garnish* toasted coconut, *for garnish*

Wine: A demi-sec Champagne, like Laurent-Perrier Demi-Sec
Beer: An American porter, like Maui Brewing Co. Coconut Porter
Cocktail: La Perla (pg. 127)

ALMOND TEA CAKE
BISTRO ALEX, HOTEL SORELLA

Located in the Hotel Sorella in West Houston's CityCentre, Bistro Alex is part of the Brennan's family of restaurants. Although menus include many of Brennan's classic dishes, such as their famous turtle soup, Chef Roland Soza also features many seasonally focused dishes and small plates. Their New Orleans-style jazz brunch on Sundays features live entertainment and bottomless mimosas.

Recipe Note: Pastry Chef Rosa Ortez says not to worry if blueberries aren't in season, the compote can be made with other types of seasonal berries and fruit.

CAKE

½ lb	unsalted butter
1 cup	granulated sugar
6 oz	almond paste
½ Tbsp	vanilla extract
5	eggs
1 cup	all-purpose flour
½ tsp	baking powder

BERRY COMPOTE
Makes 2 cups

2 cups	fresh blueberries
⅓ cup	granulated sugar
2 Tbsp	Limoncello (Italian lemon-flavored liqueur)
	freshly whipped cream
sprinkle	powdered sugar
	mint sprig, *for garnish*

YIELD: 1 BUNDT CAKE

For the cake:

Preheat the oven to 325˚F.

In a stand mixer fitted with a paddle attachment, cream the butter, sugar and the almond paste. Add the vanilla extract and then add the eggs, one at a time.

Sift the flour and baking powder and add to the sugar mixture.

Bake for 35 to 45 minutes, or until a toothpick or skewer inserted into the cake comes out clean. Allow the cake to cool.

For the berry compote:

In a medium bowl, mix the berries with the sugar and limoncello, allow mixture to macerate.

To serve:

Cut the cooled cake into ½-inch slices. Top a slice of cake with berry compote, whipped cream and another slice of cake. Sprinkle with powdered sugar and garnish with a mint sprig.

Wine: A demi-sec Champagne
Beer: A fruity witbier, like Samuel Adams Blackberry
Cocktail: Classic Mojito (pg. 123)

BUTTERSCOTCH TARTS
BRASSERIE 19

Chef Amanda McGraw is so fond of the Belgian beer Trappistes Rochefort, she created this tart specifically to pair with it. If ever there was a perfect pairing – this is it!

Recipe Notes: Be sure to use Jack Daniels or Maker's Mark in the custard. Sheet gelatin may be purchased locally at Central Market or online.

YIELD: SIX (4-OUNCE) TARTS

For the tart shells:

Preheat the oven to 350˚F. Mix all of the ingredients in a medium bowl. Press into greased tart pans. Chill for 30 minutes. Bake for about 15 to 18 minutes.

For the chocolate layer:

Combine the dark chocolate and heavy cream in a small saucepan or double boiler. Melt over medium heat; mix until smooth. Remove from heat and pour the chocolate into the baked tart shells to evenly cover the bottom. Chill for at least 20 minutes or until hardened.

For the butterscotch pudding:

Lightly brown the butter in a medium saucepan over medium heat. Add the dark brown sugar and the salt. Melt together, then remove from the heat. In a bowl, whisk together the cornstarch, milk and eggs. Slowly temper the milk mixture into the butter mixture. Return to high heat and bring to a boil while whisking constantly. Reduce heat to medium-high and continue to whisk, until thickened, approximately 15 minutes. Remove from the heat. Add in the whiskey, vanilla extract, molasses and gelatin and whisk until smooth. Pour into a shallow pan and place in the refrigerator to chill.

To serve:

Fill each tart shell with butterscotch pudding. Garnish with chopped chocolate toffee pieces.

TART SHELLS

2½ cups	pecans, toasted and ground
¼ tsp	cinnamon, ground
⅓ cup	granulated sugar
1 tsp	kosher salt
6 Tbsp	unsalted butter, browned

CHOCOLATE LAYER

4 oz	dark chocolate
½ cup	heavy cream

BUTTERSCOTCH PUDDING

6 Tbsp	unsalted butter
1½ cups	dark brown sugar
¾ tsp	salt
5 Tbsp	cornstarch
3¾ cups	milk
3	eggs, whisked
2 Tbsp	whiskey
2 Tbsp	vanilla extract
1 Tbsp	molasses
10	gelatin sheets, 2½- by 4½-inch, bloomed in ice water
	chopped chocolate toffee bar, *for garnish*

Wine: A late harvest Pinot Gris
Beer: A Belgian ale, like Trappistes Rochefort
Cocktail: Royal Mission (pg. 134)

LEMON SEMIFREDDO
COPPA RISTORANTE ITALIANO

Executive Chef Brandi Key reinvents classic Italian dishes using local ingredients at Coppa, the newest restaurant by the ever-expanding Clark Cooper Concepts group. Attention to detail is apparent in every dish – she makes as much as possible from scratch daily.

Recipe Note: No double boiler? A stainless steel mixing bowl that will fit on top of a saucepot without touching the water will work just as well.

YIELD: FOUR (6-OUNCE) SERVINGS

LEMON CURD

6	egg yolks
1⅓ cups	granulated sugar
3 Tbsp	fresh lemon juice
3 oz	unsalted butter, chilled and diced

LEMON SEMIFREDDO

1 cup	heavy cream, very cold
1 cup	lemon curd, cold

PISTACHIO CRUNCH

½ cup	granulated sugar
2 Tbsp	water
½ cup	raw pistachios, shelled

For the lemon curd:

Heat water in the bottom of a double boiler over medium-high heat, bring to a boil, then reduce to medium-low. Combine the egg yolks and sugar in top of the double boiler. Using a hand mixer, whisk the egg yolks and sugar on medium speed until smooth. Add the lemon juice and whisk to combine. Place the bowl on top of the double boiler and whisk constantly until the mixture thickens and doubles in volume, 8 to 10 minutes. Remove from the heat and whisk in the butter, a few pieces at a time, until completely incorporated. Transfer the lemon curd to a new stainless steel bowl, cover with a piece of plastic wrap (make sure the plastic wrap touches the curd; this keeps a skin from forming) and cool completely in the refrigerator.

For the lemon semifreddo:

Whip the heavy cream in the chilled bowl of a stand mixer with a whisk attachment on medium-high until doubled in volume (soft peaks). Add the whipped cream to the lemon curd and whisk gently. Spray the ramekins with cooking spray. Using an ice cream scoop, divide the mixture between the ramekins. Tap the ramekins lightly to flatten the tops of the semifreddo. Cover with plastic wrap and transfer to the freezer. Allow to set overnight.

For the pistachio crunch:

Place the sugar and water in a stainless steel saucepan over medium-low heat. Allow the sugar to melt, without stirring, until completely dissolved. When the sugar starts to turn light golden brown, add the pistachios, and stir with a wooden spoon to evenly coat. The mixture will immediately seize up, but keep stirring. Transfer to a sheet pan lined with a silicone mat or parchment paper, and allow to cool to room temperature. Once cool and hard, place the pistachio crunch on a cutting board, and coarsely chop with a knife. Store covered at room temperature.

To serve:

Fill a bowl with hot tap water; set aside. Place a spoonful of the lemon curd on a plate then use the back of the spoon to smear the curd across the plate.

Remove a lemon semifreddo from the freezer and dip the bottom of the ramekin into the hot water to loosen. Turn the ramekin upside down on the plate in the lemon curd and gently shake until the semifreddo releases onto the plate. Sprinkle the pistachio crunch over the top of the semifreddo and onto the plate. Serve immediately.

Wine:	A French apéritif, like Lillet Blanc, garnished with an orange slice
Beer:	A wheat ale, like Karbach Weisse Versa Wheat
Cocktail:	B$_2$ (pg. 139)

WHITE CHOCOLATE MACADAMIA COOKIES
DESSERT GALLERY BAKERY & CAFÉ

Pastry Chef Sara Brook has loved desserts since the day she was born. She's been baking since the age of four and still has an Easy Bake Oven in her office today.

With a huge selection of cakes, pies and cookies, Dessert Gallery is sure to satisfy your sweet tooth – their carrot cake is one of the best in town (the recipe is in my Houston Classic Desserts cookbook).

Recipe Note: For a variation, swap out the white chocolate for dark and the macadamia nuts for pecans or walnuts.

YIELD: 24 COOKIES

For the cookies:

In a stand mixer fitted with a paddle attachment, combine the butter, sugars, vanilla extract and salt. Beat until light and fluffy, about 5 minutes.

Beat in the eggs, one at time, and also the baking soda. Stir in the flour, being careful not to over-mix. Fold in the white chocolate chips and macadamia nuts.

Refrigerate until very firm (for a few hours-overnight is okay). Scoop dough into balls onto a parchment paper-lined cookie sheet. Bake at 350°F for 12 to 15 minutes or until golden brown.

For the dipping chocolate:

In a small microwave-safe bowl, combine the chopped white chocolate and the coconut oil or shortening. Place the bowl in the microwave, and cook on 70% power for 20 seconds, stir and repeat, until melted.

Dip each cookie half-way into the chocolate, then place on a parchment paper-lined sheet pan. Place in the refrigerator to harden.

COOKIES

⅔ cup	unsalted butter, softened
⅔ cup	brown sugar
⅓ cup	granulated sugar
½ Tbsp	vanilla extract
⅔ tsp	salt
5 Tbsp	egg, beaten
⅔ tsp	baking soda
2 cups	all-purpose flour
½ cup	white chocolate chips
¾ cup	macadamia nuts, chopped

DIPPING CHOCOLATE

4 oz	white chocolate bar, chopped
1½ tsp	coconut oil or shortening

Wine: A Moscato d'Asti or a demi-sec Champagne
Beer: An American strong ale, like Abita Vanilla Doubledog
Cocktail: The Duffy (pg. 141)

Three Blind Mice Punch
Brooklyn Athletic Club

Rum punch or pum runch?

Call it what you like but if asked to make a second batch, just remember this age-old recipe/rhyme: "One of sour, two of sweet, three of strong, four of weak." Modern translations include using juice (instead of water) for the weak and liqueurs such as the nutmeg-flavored Dram in this recipe.

2 oz	Smith & Cross Jamaican Rum
¼ oz	St. Elizabeth Allspice Dram
	(allspice liqueur)
2 oz	fresh pineapple juice
2 oz	fresh orange juice
½ oz	fresh lime juice
1 oz	Agave Syrup (pg. 142)
splash	grenadine
	fresh pineapple, *for garnish*
	fresh cherry, *for garnish*

Fill a cocktail shaker with ice. Add all of the ingredients except for the garnish; shake until chilled. Strain into a hurricane glass. Garnish with pineapple and a cherry.

G'Vine, Lillet & Croquet!
Brooklyn Athletic Club

G'Vine is French gin that's made from the same grapes used to make cognac. Spices like ginger and cardamom along with the essence of grape blossoms make it very floral and a little spicy, with light juniper notes.

My friend, Marcy Jimenez, introduced me to G'Vine, and we were fast friends. Pick up a bottle (or two) at Houston Wine Merchant.

2 oz	Lillet Rose
2 oz	fresh grapefruit juice
1¼ oz	G'Vine gin
	Champagne, *to top*
	lemon wheel or fresh berries,
	for garnish

Fill a cocktail shaker with ice. Add all of the ingredients, except for the Champagne and garnish; shake hard, until chilled. Strain into chilled flutes or martini glasses. Top with Champagne. Garnish with a lemon wheel or fresh berries.

Lower 9th Iced Tea
BLU - Todd Leveritt

Long Island Iced Tea — Southern Style! Absolut Wild Tea vodka is made from a combination Chinese oolong tea and Scandinavian elderflower. It's also delicious on the rocks with fresh lime juice and just a splash of agave syrup.

1½ oz	Absolut Wild Tea vodka
½ oz	Wray & Nephew White
	Overproof Rum
1 oz	fresh lemon juice
1 oz	Simple Syrup (pg. 142)
dash	mint bitters
dash	Vieux Carre Absinthe
4 to 5	mint leaves
	lemon wheel, *for garnish*

Fill a cocktail shaker with ice. Add all of the ingredients; shake long and hard enough to bruise the mint. Pour into a tall glass. Garnish with a lemon wheel.

Basilini
Arturo's Uptown Italiano

8 oz	Grey Goose vodka
¼ oz	basil (about 8 leaves)
½	lime
½	lemon
1 Tbsp	granulated sugar

Muddle all of the ingredients in a cocktail shaker; let sit for 30 minutes at room temperature. Add ice; shake hard until chilled. Serve up, in martini glasses. Makes 2 cocktails.

Lemon Basil Gimlet
benjy's

1½ oz	Hudson Ferus Vodka
1 oz	Ginger Lemon Simple Syrup (pg. 142)
1¼ oz	fresh lemon juice
4	basil leaves

Fill a cocktail shaker with ice. Add the vodka, Ginger Lemon Simple Syrup, lemon juice and 3 basil leaves; shake hard until chilled. Strain into a martini glass. Garnish with the remaining basil leaf.

Southern Hospitality
Hugo's - Sean Beck

Mixologist master Sean Beck created this drink specifically to pair with Killen's Steakhouse's Duck Confit Tostadas.

Dating back to 1559, Lambics are Belgian beers produced by spontaneous fermentation using wild yeast.

¾ oz	fresh lemon juice
½ oz	Siembra Azul Blanco tequila
½ oz	Beefeater gin
3 oz	Lindemans Pêche Lambic beer
	raw sugar, *to rim glass*
	thyme sprig, *for garnish*
	lemon twist, *for garnish*

Dip the rim of apéritif glass or a Champagne flute into lemon juice and then into the sugar.

Fill a cocktail shaker with ice. Add the lemon juice, tequila and gin; shake until chilled. Strain into the sugar-rimmed glass. Slowly pour the Pêche Lambic over the top. Garnish with a thyme sprig and a lemon twist.

Negroni Sbagliato
Mongoose versus Cobra

Ah, the mistaken Negroni. The story goes that a bartender accidentally grabbed the sparkling wine instead of the gin, which is normally used in a Negroni, and the refreshing Negroni Sbagliato was born!

1 oz	Campari (bitter Italian apéritif)
1 oz	Italian sweet vermouth
2 oz	dry Prosecco, *to top*
	orange twist, *for garnish*

In a mixing glass, combine the Campari and vermouth; stir. Pour into an ice-filled glass; add the Prosecco. Garnish with an orange twist.

Rusty Cross
Down House

Complex and full flavored, Smith & Cross Traditional Jamaican Rum is 57% alcohol by volume, the proof required by the British Royal Navy. The "navy strength" rum" was used for trading purposes, but most important, if spilled onboard, would not prevent gunpowder from igniting!

1 oz	Smith & Cross Jamaican Rum
1 oz	Drambuie (malt whisky liqueur)
½ oz	St-Germain elderflower liqueur
½ oz	fresh lime juice
2 dashes	Angostura bitters
½ tsp	Chili Tincture* (pg. 142) lime wheel, *for garnish*

Fill a cocktail shaker with ice. Add all of the ingredients, except the garnish; shake until chilled. Strain into a glass. Garnish with a lime wheel.

*You can substitute Thai chili seeds or crushed red pepper for the tincture — not quite the same, but close!

Queen's Park Swizzle
Anvil Bar & Refuge

This recipe was adapted from the classic Queen's Park Swizzle from the Queen's Park Hotel in Trinidad from the 1920s.

1	turbinado sugar cube
8	mint leaves
¾ oz	Turbinado Syrup (pg. 142)
2 oz	dark rum, preferably a Demerara rum
¾ oz	fresh lime juice
3 dashes	Angostura bitters lime wedge, *for garnish* mint sprig, *for garnish*

Muddle the sugar cube in a collins glass. Add the mint and Turbinado Syrup; gently muddle. Add the rum, the lime juice and crushed ice; mix with a swizzle stick until the outside of the glass is frosted. Top with the bitters. Garnish with a lime wedge and a mint sprig.

Flaming Ladder of Death
Anvil Bar & Refuge

This cocktail was created by former bartender Peter Jahnke — it's now a house recipe that can always be made at the bar.

¾ oz	Jamaican rum
¾ oz	Black Strap rum
¾ oz	fresh orange juice
½ oz	fresh pineapple juice
½ oz	fresh lime juice
½ oz	grenadine
1 dash	Angostura bitters
3	pineapple leaves, *for garnish*
1	orange wheel, *for garnish*
1 tsp	overproof rum, *for garnish*
1	brown sugar cube, *for garnish*

Fill a cocktail shaker with ice. Add all of the ingredients except for the overproof rum and garnishes; shake well. Strain into a large Tiki mug, filled with crushed ice. Garnish with pineapple leaves and an orange wheel. Pour the overproof rum on the sugar cube and light on fire, if desired.

Hemingway's Daiquiri
Hearsay Gastro Lounge

Ernest Hemingway was said to have enjoyed this cocktail at the El Floridita Bar in Havana during his frequent visits to Cuba.

1½ oz	Bacardi rum (white)
¼ oz	Luxardo Maraschino liqueur
1 oz	fresh grapefruit juice
¾ oz	fresh lime juice
¾ oz	Simple Syrup (pg. 142)
	grapefruit wedge, *for garnish*

Fill a shaker halfway with ice. Add all of the ingredients except for the garnish; shake until chilled. Strain into a wine glass. Garnish with a grapefruit wedge.

Classic Mojito
Bistro Alex

Mojitos were first served in 1942 at La Bodeguita del Medio, a Havana, Cuba bar and restaurant frequented by celebrities like Ernest Hemingway.

3	lime wedges
5 to 6	fresh mint leaves
1½ oz	Bacardi rum (white)
¾ oz	Simple Syrup (pg. 142)
splash	club soda

In a shaker, muddle the lime wedges and the mint until aromatic. Add ice, the rum, Simple Syrup and a splash of soda. Turn over in the shaker to mix the ingredients. Pour into a rocks glass.

Fifteen Hundred Dollars & Two Weeks Off
Double Trouble

Robin Berwick and Robin Whalen were Poison Girls and now they're Double Trouble serving caffeine and cocktails!

¾ oz	Flor de Caña Gold aged rum
¾ oz	Luxardo Maraschino liqueur
¾ oz	pineapple juice
¾ oz	fresh lime juice
long dash	Angostura bitters
1 tsp	Tahitian Grenadine (pg. 142)
	lime wheel, *for garnish*
	paper umbrella, *for garnish*

Fill a cocktail shaker with ice. Add all of the ingredients except the garnishes; shake until chilled. Strain into an ice-filled rocks glass. Garnish with a lime wheel and a paper umbrella.

Manhattan
Glass Wall

This American classic was first requested at New York's Manhattan Club in 1874.

2 oz	rye whiskey
½ oz	sweet vermouth
2 dashes	Angostura bitters
	maraschino cherry, *for garnish*

Fill a cocktail shaker with ice. Add all of the ingredients except for the garnish; shake untill chilled. Strain into a chilled glass. Garnish with a cherry.

Harvard - Russell Thoede

2 oz	brandy
½ oz	Antica Formula Vermouth
½ oz	maraschino liqueur
1 dash	Angostura bitters
	orange wheel, *for garnish*
	maraschino cherry, *for garnish*

Fill a cocktail shaker with ice. Add all of the ingredients except for the garnish; shake until chilled. Strain into a chilled cocktail glass. Garnish with an orange wheel and a cherry.

1753
Masraff's

1753? You guessed it: Masraff's address on Post Oak Boulevard. I like this drink topped with a little Prosecco!

1½ oz	Cinco Vodka
½ oz	St-Germain elderflower liqueur
¾ oz	Simple Syrup (pg. 142)
½ oz	fresh lime juice
splash	fresh lemon juice
⅛ oz	balsamic vinegar
2	strawberries
	crushed black pepper, *for garnish*

Fill a cocktail shaker with ice. Add all of the ingredients, except for the garnish. Shake vigorously for 30 seconds. Strain and serve up in a martini glass. Garnish with a little crushed black pepper.

Sachin Tendulkar
The Queen Vic Pub

This cocktail is named after The Queen Vic's favorite cricket player!

1½ oz	Earl Grey Lavender Tea-Infused Vodka (below)
1 Tbsp	Honey Syrup (pg. 142)
½ oz	St-Germain elderflower liqueur
1 oz	fresh lemon juice
	lemon wheel, *for garnish*

In a cocktail shaker, stir the Honey Syrup into the vodka until it dissolves. Add the St-Germain and lemon juice and shake. Strain into a crushed ice-filled rocks glass. Garnish with a lemon wheel.

To make the Tea Vodka: In a jar, combine 1 liter of vodka with 2 Earl Grey Lavender Tea bags. Let stand at room temperature for 15 minutes (or longer, depending on desired strength. You can dilute the tea flavor with more vodka if it's too strong). Remove tea bags and store covered. (Leftover infused vodka can be kept at room temperature for up to 1 month).

Argentini
Oporto Food & Wine Bar

Primo vodka, reportedly the first-ever single-grape vodka, has been taking the globe by storm, winning a silver medal in 2007 at the International Wine and Spirits Competition in England – or less than half a year after its debut.

2 oz	Primo Vodka
½ oz	fresh lime juice
½ oz	Simple Syrup (pg. 142)
	Malbec wine, *to float*

Fill a cocktail shaker with ice. Add the vodka, lime juice and Simple Syrup; shake until chilled. Strain into a chilled cocktail glass. Using the back of a spoon, float just enough wine to cover the top of the drink.

Jalapeño Martini
Americas

Made from midwestern American grains and California's Sierra Mountain spring water, Hudson Ferus Vodka is a Texas based, all-American vodka. Gloves are always a good idea when handling fresh jalapeños!

3 to 4	fresh jalapeño slices
1	lime, juiced
1	orange wedge, squeezed
1 oz	olive juice
2 oz	Hudson Ferus Vodka
	jalapeño slice, *for garnish*

Muddle the jalapeño slices and citrus juices in a cocktail shaker. Add ice, the olive juice and vodka; shake until chilled. Strain into a cocktail glass. Garnish with a jalapeño slice.

Vesper
The Queen Vic Pub

Lillet Blanc was made famous when James Bond used the apéritif as an ingredient in his Vesper cocktail in the movie "Casino Royale." Looking for a little excitement? Light the orange peel on fire.

1½ oz	Dripping Springs Vodka
¾ oz	Waterloo Gin
¾ oz	Lillet Blanc (fortified French apéritif)
	orange peel, *for garnish*

Fill a cocktail shaker with ice. Add the vodka, gin and the Lillet. Stir, then strain into a chilled cocktail glass. Garnish with an orange peel.

Tradewinds
Coppa Ristorante Italiano - Kris Sowell

Named Food & Wine Magazine's 'Best New Vodka of 2009,' Prairie is a certified organic, kosher and gluten-free vodka, made from Minnesota corn.

1½ oz	Prairie vodka
½ oz	Hum liqueur (spiced hibiscus liqueur)
1 oz	Simple Syrup (pg. 142)
½ oz	fresh lime juice
1 dropper	Burlesque Bitters
	ginger beer, *to top*
	lime wheel, *for garnish*
	preserved hibiscus flower, *for garnish*

Fill a cocktail shaker with ice. Add all of the ingredients, except the ginger beer and garnish; shake until chilled. Pour into a collins glass. Add more ice, if needed and top with ginger beer. Garnish with a lime wheel and a hibiscus flower.

Norhill
Liberty Kitchen

Austin-based Republic Spirit Blends are all-natural, preservative-free cocktail mixes made from fresh fruit and agave nectar. They may be purchased locally at Spec's and Whole Foods.

1½ oz	Tito's Handmade Vodka
2 oz	Republic Spirit Blends Jalapeño-Lime juice
4 to 5 oz	wheat beer
	lime wedge, *for garnish*

Combine the vodka and the jalapeño-lime juice in pint glass. Fill with crushed ice; top with beer. Garnish with a lime wedge.

Katsuya Fresh
Katsuya

This refreshing cucumber and lime martini is Katsuya's signature drink!

3	cucumber slices
1½ oz	Grey Goose vodka
½ oz	Rock Saké Junmai Daiginjo sake
¾ oz	fresh lime juice
¾ oz	Simple Syrup (pg. 142)
	cucumber slice, *for garnish*

Muddle all of the ingredients except the garnish in a cocktail shaker. Fill the shaker with ice; shake until chilled. Strain into a martini glass. Garnish with a cucumber slice.

Breath of Fresh Pear
Del Frisco's Double Eagle Steakhouse

You'll want to make a pitcher of these to serve at your next brunch.

2½ oz	Grey Goose La Poire vodka
1 oz	Cointreau (orange liqueur)
1¾ oz	white cranberry juice
2	lime wedges, squeezed
	pear wheel, *for garnish*

Fill a cocktail shaker with ice. Add all of the ingredients except the garnish; shake until chilled. Strain into a martini glass. Garnish with a thin pear wheel.

Flamingo
Julia's Bistro

Subtle fruitiness of dragon fruit and papaya balance the fresh, floral notes of white grapes, in Absolut Gräpevine, their newest flavor, introduced in early 2012. All-natural ingredients and no added sugar made me an instant fan!

1½ oz	Absolut Gräpevine vodka
2 oz	fresh orange juice
½ oz	mango rum
splash	grenadine
	maraschino cherry, *for garnish*

Fill a cocktail shaker with ice. Add all of the ingredients except the garnish; shake until chilled. Strain into a rocks glass. Garnish with a maraschino cherry.

La Perla
Coppa Ristorante Italiano - Kris Sowell

That's right – La Perla, like the lingerie. It's sexy, grown-up coconut limeade.

1½ oz	Cîroc Coconut vodka
½ oz	Simple Syrup (pg. 142)
½ oz	fresh lime juice
	coconut water, *to top*
	lime wheel, *for garnish*

Combine the vodka, simple syrup and lime juice in a mixing glass. Pour over crushed ice in a rocks glass. Top with coconut water. Garnish with a lime wheel.

Western Dreamer
Remington Bar, St. Regis Hotel
Harry Spitzer

The Rangpur lime, a mandarin orange-lemon hybrid, helps give Tanqueray Rangpur gin its distinctive taste – along with a mix of juniper, bay leaf and other garden delectables.

1¼ oz	Tanqueray Rangpur gin
¼ oz	St-Germain elderflower liqueur
2 to 3 oz	ginger ale
½ oz	fresh lime juice
	lime wedge, *for garnish*

Fill a cocktail shaker with ice. Add all of the ingredients except for the garnish; shake until chilled. Pour into a chilled cocktail glass. Garnish with a lime wedge.

Jersey Mule
Vic & Anthony's Steakhouse

8	fresh mint leaves
½ oz	Simple Syrup (pg. 142)
1½ oz	Hendrick's Gin
½ oz	fresh lime juice
2 oz	ginger beer
	mint sprig, *for garnish*

In a mixing glass, muddle the mint and Simple Syrup. Fill the glass with ice. Add the gin and lime juice. Pour into a tall glass. Top with ginger beer. Stir 10 times. Garnish with a mint sprig.

Gin Gin Mule
Trevisio

5	fresh sage leaves, rolled
½ oz	fresh lime juice
½ oz	Simple Syrup (pg. 142)
2 oz	gin
	ginger beer, *to top*
	sage leaf, *for garnish*

In a cocktail shaker, gently muddle the sage, lime juice and Simple Syrup. Add ice and gin; shake until chilled. Pour into a cocktail glass; top with ginger beer. Garnish with a sage leaf.

Aviation
Mongoose versus Cobra

The Aviation is a classic cocktail made with gin, maraschino liqueur, lemon juice and crème de violette, although some recipes omit the violette liqueur. The violette brings additional sweetness, depth of flavor, and the pretty sky-colored hue, but be warned: a little goes a long way.

1½ oz	Old Tom Gin
2 tsp	Luxardo Maraschino liqueur
¾ oz	fresh lemon juice
2 tsp	crème de violette

Fill a cocktail shaker with ice. Add all of the ingredients; shake until chilled. Strain into a chilled coupe.

Gin Blossom
Glass Wall

Domaine de Canton liqueur is made from fresh baby Vietnamese ginger that's macerated with herbs and spices.

1¼ oz	Hendrick's Gin
¼ oz	St-Germain elderflower liqueur
¼ oz	Domaine de Canton (ginger liqueur)
½ oz	fresh lemon juice
2	fresh basil leaves
dash	Agave Syrup (pg. 142)
	cucumber slices, *for garnish*

In a cocktail shaker, combine the liquor and liqueurs. Add the basil and muddle. Add agave nectar, to taste. Add ice; shake until chilled. Pour into a cocktail glass. Garnish with cucumber slices.

Lemon Hat - Truluck's

1¼ oz	Tanqueray gin
	San Pellegrino Limonata, *to fill*
	lemon wedge, *for garnish*

Fill a glass with ice. Add the gin; fill with Limonata. Garnish with a lemon wedge.

Gin & Jazz
RDG + Bar Annie

The first Texas-based gin, Roxor Artisan Gin is a collaboration between Dripping Springs vodka and James Beard award-winning chef Robert Del Grande, who also happens to be a biochemist. His blend of twelve Texas botanicals – which include Texas grapefruits, limes, hibiscus, pecans and water from Edward's Aquifer – make for a light juniper and very fragrant gin.

1½ oz	Roxor Artisan Gin
¼ oz	Hibiscus Syrup (pg. 142)
¼ oz	fresh lime juice
¼ oz	Cointreau (orange liqueur)
	tonic water, *to top*
	Meyer lemon wheel, *for garnish*

In a shaker filled with ice, combine the gin, Hibiscus Syrup, lime juice and Cointreau. Shake well, then pour into a rocks glass. Top with a splash of tonic and garnish with a Meyer lemon wheel.

Pimm's Cup
Haven

This English classic originated in 1840 and is still the standard cocktail at British and American polo matches.

½ oz	dry gin
1 oz	Pimm's No. 1 (English gin-based apéritif)
1 oz	fresh lemon juice
½ oz	Turbinado Simple Syrup, (pg. 142)
	seltzer, *to top*
	cucumber slice, *for garnish*
	lemon wedge, *for garnish*

Fill a cocktail shaker with ice. Add all of the ingredients except the seltzer and garnishes; shake until chilled. Strain into an ice-filled collins glass. Top with seltzer. Garnish with a cucumber slice and a lemon wedge.

El Diablo
Down House

Tart and spicy, El Diablo is a classic cocktail from Trader Vic's cocktail book of 1946.

1½ oz	tequila
½ oz	Crème de Cassis (black currant-flavored liqueur)
1	lime wedge, squeezed ginger beer, *to top*

Fill a cocktail shaker with ice. Add all of the ingredients except for the ginger beer; shake until chilled. Strain into an ice-filled collins glass and top with ginger beer.

Strawberry Cucumber Margarita
El Gran Malo

Be sure to use 100% agave tequila for the infusion!

2 oz	fresh lemon juice
2 oz	fresh lime juice
½ oz	agave nectar (if needed)
2 oz	Strawberry-Infused Tequila (below)
1 Tbsp	fresh strawberries, chopped
1 Tbsp	fresh cucumber, chopped

Combine the lemon and lime juice; add agave nectar, if needed. Fill a cocktail shaker with ice. Add the citrus juices, Strawberry-Infused Tequila, strawberries and cucumbers. Shake vigorously, about 25 times. Serve in a margarita glass.

To make the Strawberry-Infused Tequila:

Combine 3 cups of washed, stemmed and cored strawberries and 1 liter of 100% blue agave tequila in an airtight container. Let sit in a cool, dry spot for 3 days. Strain and store in airtight container for up to 1 month.

Skinny Watermelon Margarita
Monarch, Hotel ZaZa

Watermelon and summer: don't they just go together perfectly?

4 to 6	fresh, seedless watermelon chunks (about 1 cup)
¼ oz	Monin's Sugar-Free Sweetener
2 oz	Patron Silver tequila
2 oz	fresh lime juice watermelon wedge, *for garnish*

Muddle the watermelon and sweetener in the bottom of a salt-rimmed glass. Fill the glass with ice, then add the tequila and lime juice. Garnish with a watermelon wedge.

El Gran Exito
Line & Lariat, Hotel ICON

Hotel ICON bartender Houston Farris created this drink for the first-ever San Antonio Cocktail Convention Competition in 2012, where the drink won 1st prize.

Velvet Falernum is a rum-based liqueur from Barbados, often used in Caribbean and tropical drinks.

6	fresh mint leaves
1½ oz	silver tequila (100% agave)
1 oz	fresh lime juice
1 oz	Velvet Falernum (clove-spiced liqueur)
dash	Angostura bitters
	mint leaf, *for garnish*

Add the mint leaves to a cocktail shaker. Fill the shaker halfway with ice. Add all of the other ingredients; shake until chilled. Strain into an iced rocks glass. Garnish with a mint leaf.

Que Me Quentas
Alba Huerta

This drink is light in flavor and body, but don't let it fool you; the name translates to "Tell me your story." Have a few of them, and you will definitely will be telling stories.

1½ oz	Siembra Azul Blanco tequila
¾ oz	Dolin Blanc vermouth
½ oz	Lillet Blanc (fortified French apéritif)
2 tsp	Aperol (bitter orange Italian apéritif)
2 dashes	orange bitters
1 tsp	agave nectar
	lemon twist, *for garnish*

Fill a cocktail shaker with ice. Add all of the ingredients except for the garnish; shake until chilled. Strain into a cocktail coupe. Garnish with lemon twist.

Skinny Margarita
El Real Tex-Mex Café

This is a refreshing margarita that won't blow your diet!

2 oz	Espolón tequila blanco
2 oz	fresh lime Juice
2 oz	Agave Syrup (pg. 142)
	lime wedge, *for garnish*

Fill a cocktail shaker with ice. Add all of the ingredients, except for the garnish; shake until chilled. Pour into an ice-filled mug. Garnish with a lime wedge.

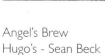

Angel's Brew
Hugo's - Sean Beck

All tequila is mezcal, but not all mezcal is tequila. Del Maguey's organic, green and sustainable mezcals have been rated the best tasting in the world for more than fifteen years.

1 oz	Del Maguey Mezcal Vida
¼ tsp	Combier Orange liqueur (orange liqueur)
1½ oz	Moscato d'Asti wine
½ oz	lime juice
3	mint leaves, rolled
1 oz	Watermelon Purée (pg. 142)
3 (1-inch)	watermelon cubes
	lime wheel, *for garnish*

In cocktail shaker, combine all of the ingredients except for the watermelon cubes and garnish. Add ice; shake until chilled. Fill a tall or collins glass with ice and the watermelon cubes. Garnish with a lime wheel.

Mezcal Buck
Mark's American Cuisine

A simple, yet tasty, drink. Mezcal affects one's palate and warms the chest, throat and mouth differently than any other alcohol.

2 oz	mezcal blanco
1 oz	fresh lime juice
4 oz	ginger beer
	lime wheel, *for garnish*

Fill a cocktail glass with ice. Add the mezcal, lime juice and top with ginger beer. Garnish with a lime wheel.

Salt of Life
Coppa Ristorante Italiano - Kris Sowell

Now, this is a Bloody Mary, folks! Mezcal lends a smokiness that you just don't get from tequila.

Shrubs are refreshing fruit and vinegar-based syrups used to make alcoholic beverages since revolutionary times.

2 oz	Nahuales mezcal
6 drops	Bittermens Hellfire Habanero Shrub
6 drops	Bittermens Orchard Street Celery Shrub
	Zing Zang Bloody Mary Mix, *to fill*
	Spicy Salt (pg. 142), *to rim glass*
	olives, *for garnish*
	lime wheel, *for garnish*
	cucumber slice, *for garnish*

Add the mezcal and shrubs to a tall collins glass rimmed with spicy salt. Top with ice; fill with bloody mary mix. Garnish with olives, and a spicy salt-dipped lime wheel and cucumber slice.

French 75 - Two Ways!
Glass Wall

The French 75 cocktail was created in 1915 at the New York Bar in Paris - which later became Harry's New York Bar. The cocktail was said to have such a kick that it felt like being shelled with the powerful French 75mm field gun. Although the classic French 75 is made with gin, some claim that it's a cognac-based drink.

2 oz	Hendrick's Gin (or cognac)
½ oz	fresh lemon juice
1 tsp	Agave Syrup (pg. 142)
	Champagne, *to fill*
	lemon twist, *for garnish*

Fill a cocktail shaker with ice. Add the gin, lemon juice and Agave Syrup; shake until chilled. Strain into a chilled Champagne flute and top off with Champagne. Garnish with a lemon twist.

Orange Crush
Glass Wall

Royal Combier is one of my favorite new discoveries. Exotic, spicy and complex, Royal Combier is not your standard orange liqueur. Jean-Baptiste Combier created this all-natural blend in 1860, which includes V.S.O.P. cognac and the most famous of all French hygienic liqueurs, Elixir Combier.

	Prosecco, *to fill*
¼ oz	Royal Combier Grande liqueur (orange liqueur)
dash	orange bitters
dash	Agave Syrup (pg. 142)
½	orange wheel, *for garnish*

Fill a chilled flute with Prosecco. Add the Royal Combier and a dash each of orange bitters and Agave Syrup. Garnish with half of an orange wheel.

Hemingway's Revenge
Absinthe Brasserie

Historically referred to in France as the "la fée verte" (the green fairy), absinthe became popular with artists, writers and poets in Paris in the 1850s. Absinthe is said to stimulate creativity but may also make you a little crazy. Van Gogh sliced off his ear in an absinthe-stoked delirium!

1½ oz	Absinthe (anise-flavored spirit)
1½ oz	Cassis liqueur (black currant-flavored liqueur)
	Champagne, *to top*

Combine the Absinthe and Cassis in a chilled Champagne flute. Top with Champagne.

Maple Old Fashioned
Backstreet Café - Sean Beck

For a traditional Old Fashioned, simply replace the maple syrup with granulated sugar and a splash of water.

2	orange slices
1	fresh cherry
2 dashes	orange bitters
2 dashes	Angostura bitters
½ oz	maple syrup
1½ oz	Maker's Mark bourbon

Gently muddle 1 orange slice with a pitted fresh cherry in a rocks glass. Add the bitters and the maple syrup; stir well. Top glass with ice and stir in the bourbon. Pour into a shaker and then right back into the rocks glass. Garnish with the remaining orange slice.

The Ambassador
Quattro, Four Seasons Hotel

Tia Maria is a coffee and vanilla-infused liqueur complemented with just a touch of Jamaican rum.

1½ oz	Knob Creek bourbon
½ oz	Tia Maria (coffee liqueur)
2 dashes	Fee Brothers Orange Bitters
	orange twist, *for garnish*

Fill a cocktail shaker with ice. Add all of the ingredients except for the garnish; shake until chilled. Strain into a chilled martini glass. Garnish with an orange twist.

Royal Mission
Brasserie 19

Mixologist Joseph Stark created this cocktail to perfectly pair with chef Amanda McGraw's Butterscotch Tart.

1 oz	Maker's Mark bourbon
1 oz	Honey Syrup (pg. 142)
1 oz	Black Mission Fig Purée, (pg. 142)
dash	orange bitters
dash	rhubarb bitters
	Champagne, *to top*
	orange twist, *for garnish*

Fill a cocktail shaker with ice. Combine all of the ingredients except the Champagne; shake until chilled. Strain into a flute. Top with Champagne. Garnish with an orange twist.

French Cowboy
Philippe - Vanessa Treviño Boyd

Full-bodied and sultry, this is Philippe's version of a Manhattan.

1¼ oz	Lillet Blanc (fortified French apéritif)
1¼ oz	Bulleit bourbon
½ oz	Citrónge (orange liqueur) orange twist, *for garnish*

Fill a cocktail shaker with ice. Add all of the ingredients; shake until chilled. Strain into a chilled cocktail glass. Garnish with an orange twist.

Whiskey Smash
Simone on Sunset

Maker's Mark goes down smooth, and the lemon and mint are a classic combination

2	sugar cubes
handful	fresh mint
1	lemon wedge
2 oz	Maker's Mark bourbon club soda, *to top* orange twist, *for garnish* fresh mint, *for garnish*

In a cocktail shaker, muddle the sugar, mint and lemon wedge into the bourbon. Strain into a rocks glass filled with ice. Top with club soda. Garnish with orange twist and fresh mint.

East Coast
Coppa Ristorante Italiano - Kris Sowell

Dating back over 265 years to 1746, Drambuie is the secret recipe of Prince Charles Edward Stuart's personal liqueur.

1 oz	Leopold Bros. Apple Whiskey
¼ oz	Drambuie 15 (Speyside malt whisky liqueur)
½ oz	Simple Syrup (pg. 142)
½ oz	fresh lemon juice
3 dashes	Bar Keep Baked Apple Bitters
1	egg white
splash	Fruit Lab Hibiscus liqueur Luxardo cherry, *for garnish*

Fill a cocktail shaker with ice. Add all of the ingredients except for the hibiscus liqueur and garnish; shake until chilled. Strain into a chilled martini glass. Slowly sink the hibiscus liqueur to the bottom. Garnish with a Luxardo cherry.

Corpse Reviver #2
Glass Wall

The Corpse Reviver and the Corpse Reviver #2 – so named because of their purported ability to bring the dead (or at least painfully hungover) back to some semblance of life – were first listed in the Savoy Cocktail Handbook in 1930.

1 oz	gin
1 oz	Lillet Blanc (fortified French apéritif)
1 oz	fresh lemon juice
1 oz	Cointreau (orange liqueur)
1 drop	Absinthe
	lemon twist, *for garnish*

Fill a cocktail shaker with ice. Add all of the ingredients except the garnish; shake until chilled. Strain into a chilled cocktail glass. Garnish with a lemon twist.

Sazerac
Mockingbird Bistro Wine Bar

The "official" Sazerac cocktail was modified in 2000 to include Sazerac Kentucky Straight Rye Whiskey.

dash	Herbsaint (anise-flavored liqueur)
3 oz	rye whiskey
¾ oz	Simple Syrup (pg. 142)
1 dash	Peychaud's Bitters
	lemon peel, *for garnish*

Place the Herbsaint in a well-chilled glass. Tilt the glass to coat sides completely and pour off excess Herbsaint. Fill a cocktail shaker with ice. Add all of the ingredients except for the garnish; shake until chilled. Strain into prepared glass. Twist lemon peel over drink and drop in gently.

Miss Taylor
Hearsay Gastro Lounge

Mark Twain said, "The true pioneer of civilization is not the newspaper, not religion, not the railroad – but whiskey!"

Glenlivet, "The single malt that started it all" is the top-selling malt whisky in the U.S. and the second-most sold single malt in the world.

1	lime
1½ oz	Glenlivet 12 (single malt Scotch whisky)
¾ oz	agave nectar
	ginger beer, *to top*
	lime twist, *for garnish*

Cut the lime in half, then squeeze and drop into a rocks glass. Top with the scotch and agave. Fill with ice and then top with ginger beer. Roll in a shaker. Garnish with a spiral-cut lime twist.

Persimmon Mint Julep
Anvil Bar & Refuge

Kinas were originally created to make quinine more palatable when given to soldiers in the malaria-plagued colonies.

6	mint leaves
2 tsp	Persimmon Syrup (pg. 142)
1 oz	Kina L'Avion D'Or (French apéritif wine)
½ oz	Daron Calvados (Normandy apple brandy)
½ oz	applejack (American apple brandy)
2 dashes	Angostura bitters
	powdered sugar-dusted mint sprig, *for garnish*

In a Julep cup, gently muddle the mint and the Persimmon Syrup. Leave the muddler in the cup and add the Kina L'Avion D'Or, Daron Calvados and the applejack. Remove the muddler, add the bitters, then the crushed ice to fill the cup halfway. Stir 20 times; add a crushed ice dome. Garnish with a powdered sugar-dusted mint sprig.

Suffering Bastard
The Queen Vic Pub

Famous bartender Joe Scialom came up with this drink at the Shepheard's Hotel in Cairo, Egypt in 1959. This concoction was popularly called a "Suffering Bastard" and, originally, a "Suffering Bar Steward," which not only magically cured a hangover, but usually started the patient on his way to a new one.

1 oz	gin
1 oz	brandy
½ oz	fresh lime juice
½ oz	Simple Syrup (pg. 142)
	ginger beer, *to fill*
	lemon wheel, *for garnish*

Combine the gin, brandy, lime juice and Simple Syrup in a tall glass. Add cubed ice and fill with ginger beer. Garnish with a lemon wheel.

Old June
Boheme

Public relations superstar Lauren Levicki turned me on to this drink – it's been a favorite ever since.

1¼ oz	Tru Organic gin
1 oz	St-Germain elderflower liqueur
1¼ oz	Simple Syrup (pg. 142)
1	lemon wedge
½ oz	fresh lemon juice
3	cucumber slices
1 pinch	ground ginger
	ginger ale, *to top*

Muddle lemons, ginger, cucumber, simple syrup and fresh lemon juice in a cocktail shaker. Add ice, the gin and liqueur; shake until chilled. Strain into a stemless wine glass or an ice-filled cocktail glass and top with ginger ale.

Where There's Smoke, There's Fire - Sangria
Hugo's - Sean Beck

This sangria can be made two days in advance – just don't add the Lambrusco until ready to serve.

I oz	Del Maguey Vida mezcal
I oz	Siembra Azul Blanco tequila
I oz	orange liqueur
9 oz	Peach Purée (pg. 142)
4 oz	Jumex Apricot Nectar
4 oz	fresh orange Juice
2 oz	fresh lime Juice
2 oz	Simple or Agave Syrup, (pg. 142)
2 oz	Odawalla Mango Tango
I	peach, sliced
I	lime, sliced
I	orange, sliced
I btl	Lambrusco wine
	peach slice, *for garnish*
	lime slice, *for garnish*
	orange slice, *for garnish*

Combine all of the ingredients except the garnishes in a large pitcher. Serve in ice-filled wine glasses, rocks glasses or mason jars. Garnish with a skewered slice of peach, lime and orange.

White Wine Peach Sangria
BRC

Perfect for parties, picnics or a day by the pool – this is just one of several tasty sangrias served at the BRC.

I cup	Peach Purée (below)
2½ L	Chablis wine (3⅓ bottles)
I cup	Simple Syrup (pg. 142)
2 cups	apple juice
	orange wheel, *for garnish*

Add all of the ingredients except for the garnish in a pitcher; stir to combine. Chill mixture for at least an hour. Serve over crushed ice. Garnish with an orange wheel.

To make the Peach Purée:

Peel the peaches and remove the pits; purée in a blender with a small amount of water.

Purple Mule
BLU - Todd Leveritt

Made for Texas summers, this is a fruity rendition of the classic Moscow Mule.

10	fresh blueberries
6	fresh raspberries
½ oz	raspberry liqueur
I½ oz	Deep Eddy or Tito's Handmade Vodka
	ginger beer, *to fill*
	fresh berries, *for garnish*

Muddle the berries into the liqueur in a cocktail shaker. Add the vodka and fill with ice; shake until chilled. Strain into an ice-filled rocks glass. Fill with ginger beer; stir gently and garnish with berries.

Summer Collins
Coppa Ristorante Italiano - Kris Sowell

Mixologist Kris Sowell's adaptation of a classic Collins drink.

1½ oz	VeeV (acai-infused spirit)
¾ oz	Campari (bitter Italian apéritif)
¾ oz	Dolin Blanc vermouth
1½ oz	fresh grapefruit juice
2 dashes	lemon bitters
½ oz	fresh lemon juice
splash	Simple Syrup (pg. 142)
splash	club soda
	grapefruit slice, *for garnish*
	thyme sprig, *for garnish*

Combine all of the ingredients except the garnishes in a collins glass; fill with ice. Top with a splash of club soda. Garnish with a grapefruit slice and a thyme sprig.

B₂
Coppa Ristorante Italiano - Kris Sowell

B.G. Reynolds' Hand-Crafted Syrups are preservative, high fructose corn syrup, and gluten-free. The passion fruit syrup will add dimension to your desserts and exotic flavor to a smoothie!

1 oz	Dolin Blanc vermouth
1 oz	Bols Barrel-Aged Genever
1 oz	B.G. Reynolds' Passion Fruit Syrup
¾ oz	fresh lemon juice
2 tsp	granulated sugar
2 droppers	Bittermens Hopped Grapefruit Bitters
1	egg white
	orange twist, *for garnish*

Fill a cocktail shaker with ice. Add all of the ingredients except the garnish; shake until chilled. Strain into a chilled martini glass. Garnish with an orange twist.

Momotsuki
Uchi - Janiece Rivas

Momotsuki literally means peach moon in Japanese, although the American translation is pink moon. Peach or pink, no matter – this drink is as tasty as it looks!

½	fresh white peach, rough chopped
1 oz	Kumquat Simple Syrup, (pg. 142)
6	Candied Kumquat Slices, (pg. 142)
2½ oz	Otokoyama sake
1 can	sparkling grapefruit soda, preferably San Pellegrino Pompelmo
	micro shiso (Japanese mint), *for garnish*

In a cocktail shaker, add the peach half and smash twice with a muddler. Add the Kumquat Simple Syrup, Candied Kumquat Slices and sake. Shake vigorously for 10 to 15 seconds. Pour the mixture over ice and top with San Pellegrino Pompelmo. Garnish with micro shiso, or any kind of readily available mint.

Root Beer Float
Glass Wall

You may not remember your very first root beer float, but I guarantee you won't forget this one!

½ cup	vanilla ice cream
1 oz	Black Maker Root Beer liqueur
¼ oz	Stolichnaya Vanilla Vodka
	8th Wonder Root Beer, *to top*
drizzle	caramel syrup

Place a few scoops of vanilla ice cream into a tall glass. Pour the liqueur, vodka and root beer over the ice cream. Add a drizzle a of caramel syrup, if desired.

No Minors Milkshake
REEF

The shot glasses these milkshakes are served in are your first clue - they are definitely not for minors!

Recipe Notes: The mixture may be placed in the freezer for up to 8 hours before use. Store in an uncut pastry or plastic bag; tie shut with a rubber band or twist tie.

3 cups	Blue Bell Vanilla ice cream
1½ oz	brandy
¾ oz	Crème de Cacao (dark, chocolate liqueur)
	chocolate straws, *for garnish*

Scoop the ice cream into a blender and allow to soften. Add the brandy and liqueur; blend until smooth. Put mixture in a pastry or plastic bag. Cut a corner off the bag and pipe into shot glasses. Garnish with a chocolate straw.

Peachblow Fizz
L'Olivier - James Watkins

Acid phosphate is made from a solution of neutralized calcium, magnesium and potassium salts. It's used to bring a sour character to cocktails without adding any citrus notes (usually from lemon or lime). Tart and tingly, but not effervescent, it's sold in liquid form and may be procured locally at Houston Wine Merchant.

1½ oz	Hayman's Old Tom Gin
½ oz	Simple Syrup (pg. 142)
½	peach, rough chopped
2 tsp	acid phosphate
1 Tbsp	heavy whipping cream
	club soda, *to top*
	peach wedge, *for garnish*

In a cocktail shaker, muddle all of the ingredients except for the club soda and the garnish; shake to emulsify. Add ice; shake until chilled. Strain into a chilled collins glass and top with club soda. Garnish with a peach wedge.

Brandy Milk Punch
Backstreet Café - Sean Beck

The Christian Brothers, a religious order, started distilling brandy back in 1882 as a way to pay for the order's schools and programs.

1½ oz	Christian Brothers Brandy
splash	Praline liqueur
2¼ oz	half & half
1 Tbsp	powdered sugar (not heaping)
	freshly grated nutmeg, *for garnish*

Fill a cocktail shaker with ice. Add all of the ingredients except the garnish. Shake vigorously for 30 seconds. Strain into a martini glass. Garnish with fresh grated nutmeg.

Greyhound Slushie
Brasserie 19 - Amanda McGraw

Chef Amanda McGraw shines in the kitchen and also behind the bar! She uses locally- made Trentino Gelato's grapefruit sorbet in this slushie cocktail.

3 oz	Hudson Ferus Vodka
1 oz	Simple Syrup (pg. 142)
1½ oz	fresh grapefruit juice
splash	Aperol (bitter orange Italian apéritif)
2 scoops	grapefruit sorbet, preferably Trentino Gelato
	grapefruit wedge, *for garnish*

Fill a cocktail shaker with ice. Add the vodka, Simple Syrup, grapefruit juice and Aperol; shake until chilled. Strain into a brandy snifter. Add 2 scoops of grapefruit sorbet. Garnish with a grapefruit wedge.

The Duffy
Coppa Ristorante Italiano - Kris Sowell

Coole Swan Superior Irish Cream Liqueur is the first-ever cream liqueur to be awarded the coveted 'Best in Show Liqueur' at the highly acclaimed World Spirits Competition in San Francisco.

¼ oz	espresso
1½ oz	Tru Organic Vanilla Vodka
1½ oz	Coole Swan Irish Cream liqueur
1 Tbsp	powdered sugar
1	egg white
splash	Anchor Steam Porter beer
3 drops	Bittermens Mole Bitters
sprinkle	cinnamon sugar
	coffee beans, *for garnish*

Fill a cocktail shaker halfway with ice. Add all of the ingredients, except the bitters, cinnamon sugar and garnish; shake until chilled. Strain into a chilled martini glass, add 3 drops of bitters and sprinkle with cinnamon sugar. Garnish with coffee beans.

Always let your syrup cool before using it in drinks. Most syrups will keep for 1 month, if covered and refrigerated.

Flavors of syrups are affected by the type of sugar (refined or unrefined), agave nectar (light or dark) or honey used. For a richer syrup, use twice as much of the sweetener as water.

To make Simple Syrup:

In a small saucepan, bring 1 cup of water and 1 cup of granulated sugar to a boil over high heat, stirring until the sugar dissolves. Cool and store covered in the refrigerator.

To make Turbinado Syrup:

In a small saucepan, bring 2 cups of unrefined sugar and 1 cup of water to a boil over medium-high heat, stirring until it dissolves. Cool and store covered in the refrigerator.

To make Honey or Agave Syrup:

Place equal amounts of honey or agave nectar and water in a small saucepan and stir until dissolved. Bring to a gentle boil over medium-high heat. Reduce heat and simmer until syrup is slightly thickened, about 3 minutes. Remove from heat and let cool. Transfer syrup to a container with a tight-fitting lid, cover, refrigerate and use as needed.

You can also combine equal parts of honey or agave nectar and hot water in a jar and stir to combine.

To make Persimmon Syrup:

Dice 3 large persimmons and place in a saucepan with 1¼ cups of turbinado sugar and ⅔ cup water and bring to a boil; reduce the heat and simmer until it reaches a syrupy consistency. Strain through a fine-meshed sieve or cheesecloth into a sterilized bottle or container.

To make Tahitian Grenadine:

In a saucepot over medium-high heat, combine ½ cup of double-strength hibiscus tea, ½ cup pomegranate concentrate, 1 cup of granulated sugar, and the scraping of half of a Tahitian vanilla bean. Stir until the sugar dissolves.

To make Hibiscus Syrup:

In a stockpot, add 3 ounces of dry hibiscus flowers to a gallon of water. Boil for 3 to 5 minutes. Strain, then continue to cook over medium-high heat to reduce to half. Add granulated sugar to taste; it should have a light syrup-like texture.

To make Candied Kumquats and Kumquat Syrup:

In a saucepan over low heat, combine 1½ cups of granulated sugar, the juice of ¼ of a lemon, and 10 thinly sliced kumquats. Stir the mixture if you like, but it's not required. Let cook, swirling the pan around, until the syrup is golden in color. Turn off the heat and allow to cool. Add ½ cup hot water to the syrup, as needed for a thin, light consistency. Transfer the mixture to a covered container and store in the refrigerator.

To make Lemon Basil Simple Syrup:

Combine the zest of 1 lemon, a 3-inch piece of fresh ginger, 2 tablespoons of thyme, ⅓ of a bay leaf with 2 cups of granulated sugar and 2 cups of distilled water. Simmer for 15 to 20 minutes, then strain. Add 2 ounces of fresh basil leaves and let steep for 10 minutes. Strain to remove basil. Store covered, in the refrigerator.

To make Peach Purée:

Remove the pits from the peaches. Add the peaches, 1 ounce of fresh lime juice and 1 ounce Jumez Apricot Nectar to a blender. Purée until smooth.

To make Watermelon Purée:

Remove the rind and cut the watermelon into 1-inch cubes. Be sure to reserve enough cubes for drink garnishes. Fill a blender to the top, with watermelon cubes. Press down with your hand to release juice and then fill with more watermelon cubes. Add 2 ounces of lime juice and blend well. Run the purée through a sieve or strainer to remove the largest pulp. Store covered in the refrigerator for up to a week.

Note: This juice is fantastic in margaritas, combined with ginger beer, ice tea or it can be frozen into ice cubes for other drinks.

To make Black Mission Fig Purée:

Blend 4 ounces of dried black mission figs and stems with 8 ounces of water; then strain. Store covered in the refrigerator for up to a week.

To make Chili Tincture:

Fill a 8-ounce jar with Thai chilis. Pour high-proof spirits (at least 100 proof-can be vodka or grain liquor) over the chilis to cover. Seal the jar and wait for 2 weeks. Pour through a strainer and apply judiciously.

To make Spicy Salt:

Combine kosher salt, red chili pepper flakes, celery salt, Hatch chili pepper salt and ground cumin, to taste.

Dial up the heat with the red chili and tame the smoke with the cumin powder.

NOTES

RESTAURANT & BAR LISTINGS

Absinthe Brasserie
609 Richmond Avenue
Houston, TX 77006
(713) 528-7575
www.absinthelounge.com

Alto Pizzeria
2800 Kirby Drive
Houston, TX 77098
(713) 386-6460
www.avaalto.com

Americas
2040 West Gray Street
Houston, TX 77019
(832) 200-1492
www.cordua.com/Americas
*Other location in The Woodlands

Anvil Bar & Refuge
1424 Westheimer Road
Houston, TX 77006
(713) 523-1622
www.anvilhouston.com

Arturo's Uptown Italian
1180-1 Uptown Park Boulevard
Houston, TX 77056
(713) 621-1180
www.arturosuptown.com

Backstreet Café
1103 South Shepherd Drive
Houston, TX 77019
(713) 521-2239
www.backstreetcafe.net

benjy's
2424 Dunstan Road
Houston, TX 77005
(713) 522-7602
www.benjys.com
*Other location on Washington

Bistro Alex
Hotel Sorella
800 Sorella Court
Houston, TX 77024
(713) 827-3545
www.bistroalex.com

BLU
2248 Texas Drive
Sugar Land, TX 77479
(281) 903-7324
www.blusugarland.com

Boada Cuisine
6510 Del Monte Drive
Houston, TX 77057
(713) 782-3011
www.boadacuisine.com

Boheme
307 Fairview Street
Houston, TX 77006
(713) 529-1099
www.barboheme.com

Brasserie 19
1962 West Gray Street
Houston, TX 77019
(713) 524-1919
www.brasserie19.com

BRC Gastropub
519 Shepherd Drive
Houston, TX 77007
(713) 861-2233
www.brcgastropub.com

Brooklyn Athletic Club
601 Richmond Avenue
Houston, Texas 77006
(713) 527-4440
www.brooklyn-athletic-club.com

Concepción
819 West Alabama
Houston, TX 77006
(713) 520-7744

Coppa Ristorante Italiano
5555 Washington Avenue
Houston, TX 77007
(713) 426-4260
www.copparistorante.com

CRÚ Food & Wine Bar
2800 Kirby Drive, Suite B-130
Houston, TX 77098
(713) 528-9463
www.cruwinebar.com
*Other location in The Woodlands

Del Frisco's Double Eagle Steakhouse
5061 Westheimer Road
Houston, TX 77056
(713) 355-2600
www.delfriscos.com

Dessert Gallery Bakery & Café
3600 Kirby Drive, Suite D
Houston, TX 77098
(713) 522-9999
www.dessertgallery.com
*Other location on Post Oak

Double Trouble
3622 Main Street
Houston, TX 77006
(713) 874-0096

Down House
1801 Yale Street
Houston, TX 77008
(713) 864-3696
www.downhousehouston.com

El Gran Malo
2307 Ella Boulevard
Houston, TX 77008
(832) 767-3405
www.elgranmalo.com

El Meson
2425 University Boulevard
Houston, TX 77005
(713) 522-9306
www.elmeson.com

El Real Tex-Mex Café
1201 Westheimer Road
Houston, TX 77006
(713) 524-1201
www.elrealtexmex.com

Fluff Bake Bar @ Revival Market
550 Heights Boulevard
Houston, TX 77007
(832) 374-8340
www.fluffbakebar.com

Fuad's
6100 Westheimer Road # 144
Houston, TX 77057
(713) 785-0130

Giacomo's Cibo e Vino
3215 Westheimer Road
Houston, TX 77098
(713) 522-1934
www.giacomosciboevino.com

Gigi's Asian Bistro
5085 Westheimer Road # B2515
Houston, TX 77056
(713) 629-8889
www.gigisasianbistro.com

Glass Wall
933 Studewood Street
Houston, TX 77008
(713) 868-7930
www.glasswalltherestaurant.com

Haven
2502 Algerian Way
Houston, TX 77098
(713) 581-6101
www.havenhouston.com

Hearsay Gastro Lounge
218 Travis Street
Houston, Texas 77002
(713) 225-8079
www.hearsayhouston.com

Hugo's
1600 Westheimer Road
Houston, TX 77006
(713) 524-7744
www.hugosrestaurant.net

Hubbell & Hudson
24 Waterway Avenue, Ste. 125
The Woodlands, TX 77380
(281) 203-5600
www.hubbellandhudson.com

Jonathan's The Rub
9061 Gaylord Street
Houston, TX 77024
(713) 465-8200
www.jonathanstherub.com

Julia's Bistro
3722 Main Street
Houston, TX 77002
(713) 807-0090
www.juliasbistro.com

Katsuya
2800 Kirby Drive
Houston, TX 77098
(713) 590-2800
www.sbe.com/katsuya/houston

RESTAURANT & BAR LISTINGS

Killen's Steakhouse
2804 South Main Street
Pearland, TX 77581
(281) 485-0844
www.killenssteakhouse.com

Le Mistral
1400 Eldridge Parkway
Houston, TX 77077
(832) 379-8322
www.lemistralhouston.com

Liberty Kitchen
1050 Studewood Street
Houston, TX 77008
(713) 802-0533
www.libertykitchenoysterbar.com

Line & Lariat
Hotel ICON
220 Main Street
Houston, TX 77002
(832) 667-4470
www.hotelicon.com/dining-2/

L'Olivier
240 Westheimer Road
Houston, TX 77006
(713) 360-6313
www.lolivierhouston.com

Masraff's
1753 Post Oak Boulevard
Houston, TX 77056
(713) 355-1975
www.masraffs.com

Mark's American Cuisine
1658 Westheimer Road
Houston, TX 77006
(713) 523-3800
www.marks1658.com

MAX's Wine Dive
4720 Washington Avenue
Houston, TX 77007
(713) 880-8737
www.maxswinedive.com/houston

Mockingbird Bistro Wine Bar
1985 Welch Street
Houston, TX 77019
(713) 533-0200
www.mockingbirdbistro.com

Monarch
Hotel ZaZa
5701 Main Street
Houston, TX 77005
(713) 527-1800
www.hotelzaza.com/houston/monarch

Mongoose versus Cobra
1011 McGowen Street
Houston, TX 77002
(713) 650-6872
www.mongooseversuscobra.com

Oporto Food & Wine Bar
3833 Richmond Avenue
Houston, TX 77027
(713) 621-1114
www.oporto.us

Philippe Restaurant + Lounge
1800 Post Oak Boulevard
Houston, TX 77056
(713) 439-1000
www.philippehouston.com

MKT BAR, Phoenicia Specialty Foods
1001 Austin Street
Houston, TX 77010
(832) 360-2222
www.phoeniciafoods.com
*Multiple locations

Plonk!
1214 West 43rd Street
Houston, TX 77018
(713) 290-1070
www.plonkbistro.com

Quattro
Four Seasons Hotel
1300 Lamar Street
Houston, TX 77010
(713) 276-4700
www.quattrorestauranthouston.com

RDG + Bar Annie
1800 Post Oak Boulevard
Houston, TX 77056
(713) 840-1111
www.rdgbarannie.com

REEF
2600 Travis Street
Houston, TX 77006
(713) 526-8282
www.reefhouston.com

Remington
St. Regis Hotel
1919 Briar Oaks Lane
Houston, TX 77027
(713) 403-2631
www.starwoodhotels.com/stregis

Ristorante Cavour
Hotel Granduca
1080 Uptown Park Boulevard
Houston, TX 77056
(713) 418-1104
www.granducahouston.com/dining

Roost
1972 Fairview Street
Houston, TX 77019
(713) 523-7667

Simone on Sunset
2418 Sunset Boulevard #A
Houston, TX 77005
(713) 636-3033
www.simoneonsunset.com

Sparrow Bar + Cookshop
3701 Travis Street
Houston, TX 77002
(713) 524-6922
www.sparrowhouston.com

Sullivan's Steakhouse
4608 Westheimer Road
Houston, TX 77027
(713) 961-0333
www.sullivanssteakhouse.com/houston

TableOne
Royal Sonesta Hotel
2222 West Loop South
Houston, TX 77027
(713) 627-7600
www.sonesta.com/RoyalHouston/

The Queen Vic Pub
2712 Richmond Avenue
Houston, TX 77098
(713) 533-0022
www.thequeenvicpub.com

The Tasting Room
1101-18 Uptown Park Boulevard
Houston, TX 77056
(713) 993-9800
www.tastingroomwines.com
*Multiple locations

Tintos Spanish Restaurant & Wine Bar
2015 West Gray Street # J
Houston, TX 77019
(713) 522-1330
www.tintosrestaurant.com

Trentino Gelato
2219 Canal Street
Houston, TX 77003
(713) 444-1439
www.trentinogelato.com

Trevisio
6550 Bertner Avenue
Houston, TX 77030
(713) 749-0400
www.trevisiorestaurant.com

Truluck's
5350 Westheimer Road
Houston, TX 77056
(713) 783-7270
www.trulucks.com

Uchi
904 Westheimer Road
Houston, TX 77006
(713) 522-4808
www.uchirestaurants.com

Valentino
Hotel Derek
2525 West Loop South
Houston, TX 77027
(713) 850-9200
www.hotelderek.com/valentino

Vic & Anthony's Steakhouse
1510 Texas Avenue
Houston, TX 77002
(713) 228-1111
www.vicandanthonys.com

INDEX

INDEX

ACKNOWLEDGMENT

A question I am asked time and again is how do I get chefs and restaurants to share their recipes for my books? My answer is always the same, "I just ask nicely."

How fortunate am I to live in a city where there is so much culinary talent? And not just talent, but also graciousness?!

After all, there are few people more generous than chefs and restaurateurs. Luckily, all the mad culinary talent in Houston is balanced with award-winning sommeliers, mixologists, wine and beer professionals. It is truly a privilege and honor to work with all of them. I am constantly inspired by their relentless vision and determination to keep it fresh and interesting. To them all, I give profuse thanks.

My life of "cookbookery" brings immense joy; thanks to Kit Wohl for not only leading me down the path, but for her continued guidance and support. I am beyond blessed to have her in my life.

This book would not be near as fabulous without the many contributions of William Jones Miller, from production to photography, to photography instructor. Jeffrey Linthicum's creative talents, from graphic design to set decoration and beyond, are much appreciated. Taylor Byrne Dodge and Molly Merkle were sounding boards, therapists, tasters, testers, and editors– thanks, ladies! And then there's my self-proclaimed marketing director, Jim Veal – who always makes me feel like a rockstar – thanks, Jimmy!

Pairing assistance was immense: Thanks to Marcy Jimenez, Russell Thoede, Kris Sowell, Shepard Ross, Sean Beck, Alba Huerta, Manny Guerra, Jeff Miller, Shafer Hall, Theo Komisarjevsky and Mike Johnson. I learned so much from all of you. Of course, the Betty Ford bus is probably on its way to pick me up right about now... but it's all good.

Editorial and proofreaders: A special thanks to Jake Rigdon, who came on board in the eleventh hour– I'm sure you really don't believe that my keyboard cover is the cause of all of my errors! Also, Kim Ellis, Charles Flood, Heather Green, Diane Hause and Judy Tedrich-Henrichsen – thanks for your eyes. I am going to make an eye doctor appointment immediately!

Public relations folks: Dick Dace, Mark Hanna, Michelle LeBlanc, Katy Mayell, Paula Murphy, Katherine Orellana, Kimberly Park, Kim Padgett, Stuart Rosenberg and Mark Sullivan – thanks for all of your help and assistance.

Recipe testers and tasters were plentiful as always: Lynne Arnoff, Catherine Buchanan, Taylor Byrne Dodge, Lori Holland Dixon, Jody Rigdon, Karen Stearns, Heidi Arceneaux, Lorie Elizabeth, Elizabeth Fieldcamp, Tissie Gray, Lauren Levicki, Debbie Luby, Samira Salman and Cathi Walsh – thanks for your time, input and taste buds (and some of you provided transportation as well; you know who you are!).

Thanks to Houston Wine Merchant, Phoenicia Specialty Foods and Sur la Table, who were kind enough to lend me set decorations on multiple occasions.

Special thanks to my family, for all their support, understanding and forgiveness. I will do my best not to miss another holiday! And I can't forget my friend and personal trainer, Gustavo Ruiz - thanks, baby!

As usual, any errors or omissions are purely my doing. If you have any questions or comments, find me on Facebook or send an email to: erin@erinmhicks.com.

TABLEONE, ROYAL SONESTA • MASRAFF'S • LINE & LARIAT, HO
CUISINE • ROOST • GIACOMO'S CIBO E VINO • EL REAL TEX-MEX C
ST. REGIS HOTEL • GLASS WALL • FUAD'S • TREVISIO • LE MISTI
GRAN MALO • DEL FRISCO'S DOUBLE EAGLE STEAKHOUSE • EL
• THE TASTING ROOM • REEF • MOCKINGBIRD BISTRO WINE BA
• DOWN HOUSE • PLONK! • MARK'S AMERICAN CUISINE • CRÚ
• JULIA'S BISTRO • QUATTRO, FOUR SEASONS HOTEL • MKT E
ARTURO'S UPTOWN ITALIANO • RISTORANTE CAVOUR, HOTEL G
BAR • CONCEPCIÓN • FLUFF BAKE BAR • BACKSTREET CAFÉ • T
• BRASSERIE 19 • COPPA RISTORANTE ITALIANO • DESSERT G
HUGO'S • KATSUYA • HAVEN • RDG • HEARSAY GASTRO LOUNG
SUNSET • L'OLIVIER • MONGOOSE VERSUS COBRA • BLU • TABL
• THE QUEEN VIC PUB • JONATHAN'S THE RUB • BOADA CUISI
AMERICAS • SPARROW BAR + COOKSHOP • THE REMINGTON, S
PHILIPPE • TINTOS SPANISH RESTAURANT & WINE BAR • EL GRAI
• OPORTO FOOD & WINE BAR • VALENTINO, HOTEL DEREK • THE
ANTHONY'S STEAKHOUSE • MAX'S WINE DIVE • BENJY'S • DOWN
BAR • TRULUCK'S • KILLEN'S STEAKHOUSE • UCHI • JULIA'S BI
SPECIALTY FOODS • MONARCH, HOTEL ZAZA • ARTURO'S UPTOW
KITCHEN • GIGI'S ASIAN BISTRO & DUMPLING BAR • CONCEPCI
SULLIVAN'S • BISTRO ALEX, HOTEL SORELLA • BRASSERIE 19 •
ATHLETIC CLUB • ANVIL BAR & REFUGE • HUGO'S • KATSUYA • I
TROUBLE • HUGO'S • BRC • SIMONE ON SUNSET • L'OLIVIER • M
MASRAFF'S • LINE & LARIAT, HOTEL ICON • THE QUEEN VIC PUE
CIBO E VINO • EL REAL TEX-MEX CAFÉ • AMERICAS • SPARROW
WALL • FUAD'S • TREVISIO • LE MISTRAL • PHILIPPE • TINTOS SP.
DOUBLE EAGLE STEAKHOUSE • EL MESON • OPORTO FOOD & W
MOCKINGBIRD BISTRO WINE BAR • VIC & ANTHONY'S STEAKHOU
AMERICAN CUISINE • TRULUCK'S • KILLEN'S STEAKHOUSE •